D1296465

Rejecting Compromise

Legislative solutions to pressing problems like balancing the budget, climate change, and poverty usually require compromise. Yet national, state, and local legislators often reject compromise proposals that would move policy in their preferred direction. Why do legislators reject such agreements? This engaging and relevant investigation into how politicians think reveals that legislators refuse compromise – and exacerbate gridlock – because they fear punishment from voters in primary elections. Prioritizing these electoral interests can lead lawmakers to act in ways that hurt their policy interests and also overlook the broader electorate's preferences by representing only a subset of voters with rigid positions. With their solution-oriented approach, Anderson, Butler, and Harbridge-Yong demonstrate that improving the likelihood of legislative compromise may require moving negotiations outside of the public spotlight. Highlighting key electoral motives underlying polarization, this book is an excellent resource for scholars and students studying Congress, American politics, public policy, and political behavior.

Sarah E. Anderson is Associate Professor of Environmental Politics at the University of California Santa Barbara and University of California San Diego. Her research examines how legislatures and bureaucracies shape policy. She has previously worked as a legislative assistant for a member of Congress.

Daniel M. Butler is Professor of Political Science at the University of California, San Diego. His research uses experiments to understand representation. He is the author of *Representing the Advantaged* (Cambridge University Press, 2014).

Laurel Harbridge-Yong is Associate Professor of Political Science and a Faculty Fellow at the Institute for Policy Research at Northwestern University. Her work focus on partisan conflict and party influences. She is the author of *Is Bipartisanship Dead?* (Cambridge University Press, 2015).

Rejecting Compromise

Legislators' Fear of Primary Voters

SARAH E. ANDERSON

University of California Santa Barbara

DANIEL M. BUTLER

University of California San Diego

LAUREL HARBRIDGE-YONG

Northwestern University

CAMBRIDGE
UNIVERSITY PRESS

CAMBRIDGE
UNIVERSITY PRESS

University Printing House, Cambridge CB2 8BS, United Kingdom

One Liberty Plaza, 20th Floor, New York, NY 10006, USA

477 Williamstown Road, Port Melbourne, VIC 3207, Australia

314-321, 3rd Floor, Plot 3, Splendor Forum, Jasola District Centre, New Delhi - 110025, India

79 Anson Road, #06-04/06, Singapore 079906

Cambridge University Press is part of the University of Cambridge.

It furthers the University's mission by disseminating knowledge in the pursuit of education, learning and research at the highest international levels of excellence.

www.cambridge.org
Information on this title: www.cambridge.org/9781108738279
DOI: 10.1017/9781108768375

First published 2020
First paperback edition 2021

A catalogue record for this publication is available from the British Library

ISBN 978-1-108-48795-5 Hardback
ISBN 978-1-108-73827-9 Paperback

Contents

Figures

Tables

Acknowledgments

Writing this book has been a joy. It represents what we always imagined academia would be: discovering a puzzle, tracking down an explanation, taking intriguing detours along the way, and collaborating with colleagues who make the work seem easy. This project grew out of our shared graduate school experience. We had great advisors and a department that encouraged us to ask important questions and to use the best research to find those answers. It is not by chance that the three of us are still collaborating more than a decade after receiving our PhDs.

In bringing this book to fruition, we are grateful for so many people and organizations who made this work possible. We wish to thank the Social Science Research Council for the funding to conduct the studies that form the basis of Chapters 5 and 6. We also thank David Brady and the Hoover Institution for sponsoring a visit to bring all of the authors together for a couple of productive days of work on the manuscript.

This book leverages the insights and responses of state legislators and city officials across the country. We know how many requests public officials receive to take surveys and appreciate all of the public officials who took the time to help us with this research. We are particularly appreciative of the legislators we met through the National Conference of State Legislatures annual Legislative Summit (2016 and 2017), whose perspectives are included throughout this manuscript, and the city officials who responded to the 2016 wave of the American Municipal Official Survey. Thank you!

The book has benefited from feedback from many people over the years. We wish to thank the discussants and participants at the following conferences and seminar series (listed in alphabetical order):

- American Political Science Association (APSA) Annual Meeting (2018)
- Midwest Political Science Association Annual Meeting (2017 and 2018)
- Mini-conference on State Politics in 2015 (pre-APSA conference)
- Northwestern University
- Ohio State University
- Princeton University
- Southern Political Science Association Annual Meeting (2016)
- Stanford University
- Texas A&M University
- University of California Berkeley
- University of California San Diego
- University of California Santa Barbara
- University of Chicago
- University of Illinois, Urbana-Champaign
- University of Michigan
- University of Southern California
- University of Virginia
- Yale University

We wish to thank the people who took the time to read and comment on the full draft of the manuscript: Amanda D'Urso, Zoe Nemerever, Molly Williams, and the anonymous reviewers for Cambridge University Press. The suggestions from these individuals greatly improved the final product. We also wish to thank our editor at Cambridge University Press, Sara Doskow, who was always prompt and professional, and Kate Epstein, who carefully commented on and edited the manuscript.

Lastly, we each offer our personal thanks to those people in our lives who supported and encouraged us along the way. Sarah is grateful to her children, Ally and Cole, for being such good kids that she could write this, and for bringing her way more joy than a book could. Dan is thankful for a supportive family who made this possible. And Laurel is grateful for the support and encouragement of her husband David, who has patiently listened through the ups and downs of the research process, was always willing to be a sounding board, and celebrated each step of bringing this project to fruition.

1

Rejecting Compromise, Getting Gridlock

[Compromise is] not a 'bad' word. It's what we do in a democracy. 1/2 loaf better than no loaf. Legislation is generally incremental.
2017 NCSL Attendee 260[1]

Congress has failed to make even incremental progress on a range of pressing problems in recent decades (Binder 2014), and many Americans are frustrated by the gridlock (Newport and Saad 2016). Scholars attribute gridlock to partisan polarization, which has made it harder for legislators to find common policy ground (McCarty et al. 2006; Shor and McCarty 2011; Mann and Ornstein 2012; Binder 2014). But even on issues where agreement is possible, legislators may reject compromise proposals that move policy only partway toward their preferred outcome. Voters recognize that this type of behavior contributes to gridlock. In a 2013 Pew survey, for example, 36% of Americans thought that the main reason for inaction in Congress was that "a few members who refuse to compromise keep things from getting done" (Pew 2013). Indeed, routine rejection of what we call *half-loaf compromises* – proposals that move policy closer (but not all the way) to the legislator's preferred outcome – could be a significant contributor to legislative gridlock. Why do legislators reject such compromise offers? We find that legislators exacerbate gridlock

[1] This and the other chapter epigraphs are quotations from responses to open-ended survey questions administered to legislators and staff attending the 2017 Legislative Summit of the National Conference of State Legislatures. The attendees took a short survey and 261 attendees also filled out the optional six open-ended questions about compromise. We identify each respondent by a number between 1 and 261. Chapter 4 describes the procedures and questions in full.

by rejecting compromise proposals because they fear being punished in primary elections. In this way, legislators' electoral interests can cause them to act in ways that hurt their policy interests and may lead to representation of the uncompromising positions held by a subset of their voters at the expense of the broader electorates' preferences.

This book studies national, state, and local legislators across multiple issue domains to explore legislators' rejection of compromise proposals. To envision how the rejection of half-loaf compromises can lead to gridlock, suppose that a legislature was considering increasing the tobacco tax from a rate of $1 per pack to $1.50 because most legislators preferred the higher tax rate. Suppose, however, that many representatives who preferred a tax of $2 decided to vote against the proposal because the increase was too small. If enough legislators vote against the proposal even though it moves policy closer to what they would prefer, the legislature would fail to pass the compromise. How often do legislators reject half-loaf compromises? Why do they reject them? Can anything be done to increase legislators' ability to reach more compromises and thus overcome policy gridlock? This book investigates these questions through a problem-oriented approach that seeks to understand legislators' rejection of compromise while also providing broader insights into legislative behavior and the electoral connection.

Original surveys of both state legislators and city officials show that substantial percentages – 13% to 23% – reject half-loaf compromises. This points to an overlooked driver of legislative gridlock. Those legislators who report that their voters are likely to punish compromise are more likely to reject these half-loaf offers, suggesting that legislators' perceptions of their voters are an important element of understanding the rejection of compromise. Evidence from surveys we conducted at the National Conference of State Legislatures (NCSL) annual Legislative Summit shows that this fear of voter punishment is centered on primary voters. Consistent with this perspective, we find that Republican members of Congress with more constituents who support the Tea Party, which opposes compromise and often threatens primary challenges, are more likely to reject compromises.

The focus on legislators' beliefs that their constituents will punish them in primaries raises the question of whether their fears are justified. In survey experiments on a representative sample of the public we find that most voters, even most primary voters, reward legislators for compromising. However, co-partisan primary voters who oppose the particular compromise being offered will punish the legislator with lower approval and by voting against the legislator for supporting a half-loaf offer. In our sample, approximately a third of a legislators' primary voters fell into this punishing group. Even though legislators are likely to be electorally rewarded in both the general and primary elections for supporting compromise policies, a substantial segment of their primary electorate will punish them for voting for a compromise on a given vote. Legislators, who "run scared" in every election (Mayhew 1974), respond to the threat of punishment by rejecting compromises.

Despite the fact that only a small proportion of the electorate punishes compromise, legislators may choose to avoid angering this subset of voters in the primary election even if doing so means the legislators cannot represent the preferences of the broader electorate well. Primary voters are generally more extreme than others, may be more likely to seek out information about the issue, more likely to engage in activism, and more likely to withhold their vote because of the compromise. Thus, legislators may well fear that even a small number of such voters can yield outsized electoral consequences. While only a small number of voters might punish a legislator on a given issue, there may be many such sets of voters and many such votes. Legislators may also fear that a given compromise vote will provide fodder for a primary challenger. As a result, legislators who fear this punishment will be cautious and may often reject the compromise proposals they face. A small fraction of the primary electorate is thus shaping legislators' behavior, leading them to reject compromise proposals at the expense of representing others who do want compromise.

Given legislator perceptions of voter punishment in primaries, what types of reforms might increase legislators' willingness to compromise? In-person survey experiments with state legislators show that those assigned to consider negotiation in a private meeting report greater likelihood of compromising than those assigned to a public meeting. This suggests that there may be ways to structure negotiations that would facilitate compromise. The book concludes with a discussion of the importance of compromise for avoiding gridlock, the role of the primary electorate, and the balance between private negotiations and public representation.

THE SAN RAFAEL SWELL NATIONAL CONSERVATION AREA: A CAUTIONARY TALE

Consider the protection of public lands. The federal government owns and manages more than a quarter of the land area of the United States. How to protect these lands, while facilitating their use for recreation and natural resources, is a difficult problem that has divided citizens and policymakers alike. This issue is extremely contentious in Utah, where

63% of the land is under federal ownership. Even with the 2019 passage of an omnibus public lands bill (S. 47 in the 116th Congress) that included more than half a million acres of Utah wilderness, Utah has the least designated wilderness of any western state except Hawaii (Wilderness Connect 2019). People in Utah state politics refer to wilderness as "the W word," highlighting the contentious nature of the issue (Solomon 2016). Congressional inaction on public land management has led presidents to enter this fray, such as when President Bill Clinton created the largest national monument, Grand Staircase-Escalante, in southern Utah in 1996 and President Barack Obama created Bears Ears National Monument in the southeastern part of the state in 2017.[2]

In recent decades, the issue of public land management in Utah has become more contentious and more urgent as the growing population in Utah has brought new recreational uses like backpacking and rock climbing into conflict with older resource uses like mining and ranching. Debate over the San Rafael Swell in eastern Utah exemplifies the struggle to resolve public land management issues in a way that balances competing demands. The San Rafael Swell has deep canyons and historic petroglyphs, which highlight its natural beauty and historical connections. Bisected by Interstate 70, the Swell rises out of the desert like the geological salt dome that it once was. The increasing number of visitors to the area has damaged the petroglyphs and off-highway vehicles have produced significant damage. Use of the land for grazing and mineral extraction has sparked conflict. Backpackers objected to a stray cow in a box canyon and environmental groups opposed the opening of gypsum mines (Durrant 2007). Government employees have struggled to handle these conflicts over public land because they lacked resources. A single Bureau of Land Management (BLM) ranger patrolled the San Rafael Swell, an area the size of Connecticut.

After years of worsening problems, county commissioners, in consultation with local residents, proposed a solution – the San Rafael Swell National Conservation Area. In 2000, Congressman Chris Cannon (R-UT) introduced legislation vetted by the Secretary of the Interior to create the National Conservation Area. The conservation area designation would close the area to oil and gas exploration and leasing, shut down some off-highway vehicle trails, and offer more resources for protection.

[2] President Donald Trump subsequently halved the size of the Grand Staircase National Monument and cut Bears Ears down to 17% of its original size.

The bill seemed like a sure bet to pass, as it had support from both Democrats and Republicans, and from both federal officials and local residents. Congressman Cannon – a conservative Republican – had introduced the bill, and Bruce Babbitt, the Democratic President's Secretary of Interior, had vetted and agreed to the plan. While land use issues often pit local interests against federal interests, local support complemented federal support. The commissioners of Emery County, which contains the Swell, supported the plan, which had been developed in an extensive process of consultation with local and statewide groups. Moreover, legislators in the relevant House committee broadly agreed that action was needed; the bill passed out of the Subcommittee on National Parks and Public Lands and the Committee on Resources on voice votes (House of Representatives Resources Committee 2000).

Despite broad support for the bill, which was viewed as a compromise solution to increase protection for the Swell, it had detractors who felt it did not go far enough. The bill included environmental protections that environmental groups wanted, just not all of them. The Southern Utah Wilderness Alliance opposed the bill because it did not create full wilderness protection. Instead of imposing full wilderness designation, which would have added restrictions to how the land was used, the bill maintained the designation of much of the area as Wilderness Study Areas, which a BLM inventory process had created in the late 1970s. Some of these groups adopted "a strategy of a statewide BLM Wilderness legislation bill or nothing" (Durrant 2007, 50). Criticizing the strategy of environmental groups who would not support the bill, Molly McUsick, a legal advisor to Secretary Babbitt, declared to the *New York Times*, "Wilderness protection for a significant portion of the land is inevitable, but that's a long way down the road. Meanwhile, we think the perfect shouldn't be the enemy of the good" (Janofsky 2000).

Ultimately, the San Rafael Swell legislation failed because legislators rejected compromises that sought common ground. The initial bill was a half-loaf offer that provided more conservation than the status quo. However, legislators who wanted even more conservation pushed amendments to make it more than half a loaf. They proposed to expand the area covered, to designate the area wilderness (with the corresponding environmental protections), and to prohibit off-highway vehicles in all Wilderness Study Areas. These amendments, an effort to get more of what environmentalists wanted, alienated the original sponsors.

Representative Sherwood Boehlert (R-NY) countered these proposals with compromise substitute amendments in an effort to keep the original sponsors on board with the legislation. For example, when Representative Mark Udall (D-CO) introduced an amendment to make the Wilderness Study Areas into formal Wilderness Areas, Boehlert proposed an amendment requiring the BLM to manage the Wilderness Study Areas in at least as protective a manner as they had been previously. The substitute amendment passed 212 to 211, with the vote held open past the normal time and the Speaker of the House (who normally does not vote) casting the deciding vote.

Yet Congress rejected other compromise substitute amendments. Representative Rush Holt (D-NJ) offered an amendment to prohibit off-highway vehicles in Wilderness Study Areas, and Boehlert countered with a substitute amendment that would allow the BLM to decide this issue, saying he was trying "to seek the sensible middle ground" without "foreclos[ing] options for the future" and without "jeopardiz[ing] a very fragile, carefully crafted agreement, which has been endorsed by the Secretary of the Interior" ("Congressional Record, June 7" 2000, 3955).

When the amendment to prohibit off-highway vehicles passed without the compromise substitute amendment, Representative Cannon, the sponsor of the bill, pulled it from consideration. The legislation was dead and everyone was worse off given their preferred policy outcomes.

The failure of the San Rafael Swell National Conservation Area illustrates that legislators sometimes reject half-loaf compromises in pursuit of getting everything they want. In proposing his compromise measures Boehlert said, "Does this bill successfully dispose of every issue the way I would most prefer? No, of course not. But this is a case where an old congressional saying is quite appropriate: 'Let's not make the perfect the enemy of the good'" ("Congressional Record, June 7" 2000, 3939). It's no accident this phrase recurred in the debate; as this book will show it comes up frequently when, as in this case, compromise proposals give the negotiating parties only part of what they want. The result of failure to compromise on a National Conservation Area for the San Rafael Swell was further damage to a beautiful natural area. The Governor of Utah asked President George W. Bush to declare it a National Monument, but he declined. Subsequent BLM rules closed some of the off-highway vehicle routes proposed for closure and wilderness protection was finally included in an omnibus public lands law in 2019, but for almost twenty years the area had far fewer protections than the initial bill introduced in 2000 would have provided.

The San Rafael Swell case is not unique. In a similar scenario, conservative Republicans in both the House and the Senate expressed opposition to what was termed an "Obamacare Lite" bill in the spring of 2017, even though the proposed changes moved policy in a conservative direction (Pear and Kaplan 2017). The Patient Protection and Affordable Care Act, passed in 2010 and often called the Affordable Care Act or Obamacare, mandated that each individual have health insurance, subsidized premiums, guaranteed coverage of existing conditions, and encouraged states to expand Medicaid expansion to cover low income individuals. Repeal of Obamacare became a major rallying cry for conservatives who thought that the individual mandate went too far and that the bill interfered too much in insurance markets. The bills to repeal and replace Obamacare became known to critics as "Obamacare Lite" because they made major conservative changes to health care policy but did not fully repeal the Affordable Care Act (Cannon 2017; Demko 2017). Some conservative Republicans refused to support the compromise represented by "Obamacare Lite." As a result, the compromise did not pass even when Republicans controlled all three branches of government. But neither did the full repeal of the Affordable Care Act that these legislators sought. In 2018, Republicans repealed the individual mandate to purchase insurance through a separate piece of tax reform legislation (Paletta and Stein 2017), but many provisions opposed by Republicans, including Medicaid expansion, coverage of pre-existing conditions, and the basic structure of Obamacare remained in place. By rejecting the compromise ("Obamacare Lite") that moved health care policy closer to what they wanted (no Obamacare), conservative Republicans largely helped maintain the status quo (Obamacare).

Other examples suggest that refusing policy improvements because they do not go far enough may be common and consequential, and that it occurs at the state and local levels as well. During the reauthorization of California's cap and trade climate legislation in 2017, State Assembly member Monique Limón, who has a strong record of supporting pro-environment positions, voted against the compromise bill that provided greater environmental protections because she viewed the bill as not strong enough (Welsh 2017). And in a local example, the one city alderman who voted against a local Des Plaines, Illinois ordinance to treat vaping like smoking for those under 18 did so because he thought the proposal should apply to anyone under the age of 21 (Jordan and Burton 2018). In both of these instances, the state or local politician voted against a half-loaf compromise because it did not go far enough.

CONTRIBUTIONS TO UNDERSTANDING COMPROMISE

This book takes a problem-oriented approach by examining why legislators reject half-loaf compromises. We study what causes legislators to reject these compromises so that we can identify ways to increase legislators' willingness to compromise, helping minimize the gridlock that often paralyzes policymaking. Our results highlight how legislators' rejections of half-loaf offers exacerbate gridlock, why they reject these compromises, and how to encourage support for legislative compromise.

> Definition: Throughout the book, the terms **half-loaf offer** and **half-loaf compromise** refer to any proposals that move policy closer to, but not all the way to, the legislator's preferred outcome.

While scholars have examined how electoral environments shape voting behaviors (e.g., Canes-Wrone et al. 2002; Brady et al. 2007) and how electoral and institutional rules shape bargaining in legislatures (e.g., Baron and Ferejohn 1989; Ansolabehere et al. 2003; Volden and Wiseman 2007), much less scholarship has systematically examined legislators' support for compromise legislation. Much of the extant scholarship on legislative compromise is case-studies of notable, successful compromises (e.g., Elving 1995; Clinton and Meirowitz 2004) or treatises on the value of compromise for governing (Gutmann and Thompson 2012). We also work from the premise that compromise is often essential to governing in a democratic system but turn our focus to why individual legislators support or reject compromises that entail partial solutions. Because theories about legislative outcomes are rooted in the behavior of individuals, all of the analyses here focus on how individual legislators react to compromise proposals.[3]

Studying legislators at all levels of government – federal, state, and local – provides insights into politicians' behavior more generally. This book takes advantage of evidence from the national, state, and local levels to understand the rejection of compromise. Though there is variation across state legislatures and the federal government in factors like professionalism (Squire 2007) and the degree of majority control over the legislative

---

[3] The party is also an important unit. Indeed, party structure can give individuals incentives to take more extreme positions (Kanthak 2002; Kirkland and Harden 2016). However, other scholars have covered these dynamics effectively. We focus instead on how individual legislators have responded to half-loaf proposals.

agenda (Anzia and Jackman 2013), policymaking at all levels of government is typically viewed through the lens of rational actors making decisions based on whether they support the proposed policy over the status quo (Bertelli and Grose 2006; Crisp et al. 2011). Moreover, legislators at all levels of government face similar ranges of electoral environments, processes, and constraints (Rosenthal 2009; Trounstine 2009; Squire and Moncrief 2015). Studying compromise at these different levels of government provides general insights about politics and policymaking.

Through its range of questions, approaches, and arguments, the book makes several advances for the study of legislatures, elections, and representation. First, the book shows that rejection of half-loaf compromises is an overlooked contributor to policy gridlock. Rather than focusing on polarization – which is certainly a major driver of gridlock in contemporary politics – we show that many legislators are rejecting half-loaf compromises. This is a troubling pattern; some legislators are rejecting proposals that are in their own policy interest and contributing to gridlock in the process. While not every compromise is normatively good, finding solutions to pressing issues is an important and desirable attribute of our governance institutions.

In the aggregate, legislators' rejection of half-loaf compromises means that finding compromise solutions that benefit a majority of legislators is not always enough to achieve passage of those proposals. In the United States, most legislatures require majority support to pass a bill. Typically, this means picking policies that a majority of the legislators prefer to the status quo. However, if some legislators reject compromises that benefit them, the support of even more legislators is needed to pass a policy. This can have a big impact even if only a small number of legislators reject half-loaf offers. To illustrate, consider a proposal that would benefit 60% of a 100 person legislature. This proposal has a lot of support and should pass. However, if even 20% of legislators (i.e., 12 who would benefit from this hypothetical proposal) reject half-loaf compromises, the bill would fail despite being beneficial to a supermajority. This example highlights that even if many members support compromise proposals, the rejection of half-loaf compromises by a subset of legislators makes it even harder to pass policies in an already polarized era.

The second advance this book makes is to show that voters – and particularly primary voters – can affect legislators' willingness to compromise. We have long known that legislators are responsive to electoral concerns. Yet, scholars have often overlooked how responsiveness to particular subgroups of the electorate leads legislators to oppose policies

that make them and many of their voters – both in the general and primary electorate – better off (for exceptions, see Arnold 1990; Bishin
2000; Griffin and Newman 2005; Leighley and Oser 2017).[4] The extant
literature on retrospective voting emphasizes that voters hold legislators
accountable for their actions while in office (Key 1966; Fiorina 1983)
and electorally punish legislators who are too ideologically extreme or
too partisan (Canes-Wrone et al. 2002; Carson et al. 2010).

We uncover the common and puzzling case where legislators reject policy proposals that move policy toward their preferred outcome, even when
they are pressed to account for how voter preferences shape their own policy preferences in the first place. While legislators may have clear policy
interests, which their rejection of half-loaf compromises will harm, they
also have broader electoral interests that may be at odds with their policy
goals. This tension between policy and electoral interests contributes to
the rejection of compromise. We show that legislators' fear of punishment
in primaries drives their rejection of half-loaf compromises. Our research
thus complements scholarship on rising partisan conflict in Congress that
also emphasizes how electoral interests can work in tandem with or be in
tension with policy interests. For instance, strategic choices by party leaders to ignore bipartisan legislation or engage in messaging politics often
reflects collective electoral interests but can be at odds with individual legislators' policy interests, contributing to partisan conflict and gridlock in
the process (Harbridge 2015; Lee 2016; Koger and Lebo 2017).

We contribute to a growing literature examining the role of primaries and primary voters by showing that even relatively small subsets of
primary voters who might punish legislators electorally can shape voting behavior and policy outcomes. Past research has looked at the effect
of closed versus open primaries and found no difference (McGhee et al.
2014; McGhee and Shor 2017),[5] using this observation to conclude that
primaries have no effect. More recently, researchers have shown that this
focus on open versus closed primaries misses the point because the primary electorates in open and closed primaries do not differ appreciably.

---

[4] Much of the literature that has examined responsiveness to particular subgroups has
focused on features like aggregate congressional responsiveness to the wealthy (e.g.,
Gilens 2005; Gilens and Page 2014) or political parties' responsiveness to extreme
policy demanders in selecting stances and candidates (e.g., Bawn et al. 2012).

[5] Other work has examined how primary elections affect the selection of legislators
(Gerber and Morton 1998; Burden 2001; Kanthak and Morton 2001; Brady et al.
2007; Hall 2015).

The primary electorates in open primary states are just as extreme as those in closed primary states (Hill 2015; Norrander and Wendland 2016). In both cases, the primary electorates are representative of the parties (Sides et al. 2018), which are more extreme than the general electorate as a whole. We demonstrate an important way in which these primary electorates – whether open or closed – shape legislative behavior and policy outcomes. Legislators who fear that primary voters will punish them for compromising reject half-loaf compromises, leading to policy gridlock.

Despite legislators' perceptions, it is not clear that the electoral penalty they fear will come to pass. Most voters support compromise. In a September, 2017 Gallup poll, 54% of Americans wanted political leaders in Washington to compromise in order to get things done (Newport 2017). Our evidence suggests that voters electorally reward legislators who compromise as well. We find that even primary voters typically reward compromise votes (see Chapter 5) so legislators should generally expect to win more votes when they support compromise, even in primaries.

This does not mean that legislators have no reasons to worry. Our evidence shows that a small, committed group of primary voters who oppose a particular compromise, amounting to about one-third of co-partisan primary voters in our particular study, punish legislators for compromise. Legislators who want to ensure that they gain their party's nomination may worry that there are many such groups of voters across many issues and that these committed voters may have outsized electoral influence. As a result, legislators who fear retribution for compromise are cautious and even vote against policies that they prefer on policy terms.

In the San Rafael Swell case, fear of voter punishment in primaries was a plausible reason for the rejection of the compromise. The night before considering the amendments in Congress, members of Congress received a memo from the League of Conservation Voters declaring that the votes would be included in their year-end scorecard.[6] Members of Congress with pro-environment constituencies could expect voters to take note if they voted for the compromise substitute amendments that the League of Conservation Voters opposed. The sponsors of the legislation could also expect that their primary voters would watch it closely, as it was a local land use issue and received local and regional press coverage. In short, both sides had to worry about potential voter punishment in the primaries if they made compromises.

---

[6] http://scorecard.lcv.org/sites/scorecard.lcv.org/files/LCV_Scorecard_2000.pdf.

The third major advancement we offer here is insights into legislators' beliefs about voters and how these beliefs shape legislator behavior. The study of American politics has extensively observed legislators within their institutions and investigated the public's views of legislators. However, despite the importance of legislators' beliefs regarding their constituency to theories of legislative behavior, there is much less research that examines how legislators view their constituents (for exceptions, see Miller and Stokes 1963; Kull and Destler 1999; Broockman and Skovron 2018). To address this gap, we surveyed state legislators and city officials to understand how their beliefs about voters shape their rejection of compromise. We also rented a booth at two meetings of the National Conference of State Legislatures and conducted face-to-face surveys of legislators that allowed us to learn about their beliefs through survey questions, survey experiments and open-ended questions. We complement these elite surveys with observational studies and surveys of voters.

Through the unique lens our research methods provide, this book points to a possible means of overcoming some of the gridlock in American legislatures. Getting legislators to support half-loaf compromises requires addressing their concerns about punishment in primary elections. Private negotiations would increase the likelihood of reaching compromise by giving legislators space for discussion that is free from primary voter scrutiny and legislators' need to posture before this audience. Public (even televised) negotiations on the House floor during consideration of the San Rafael Swell bill exposed the back and forth of negotiations to the very primary voters who may have opposed and threatened to punish compromise. Structuring negotiations to allow legislators to discuss tradeoffs in private would allow them to learn about the concessions each side is willing to make without having to prematurely reveal those concessions to their primary voters. After negotiating in private, they can reveal the compromise to constituents with both the concessions and the benefits, and then face the accountability necessary for democratic representation. While this might not completely eliminate voter punishment in primaries for compromise, it could free legislators to seek solutions that would break legislative gridlock.

THE PLAN OF THE BOOK

The examples discussed above suggest that the rejection of half-loaf compromises can contribute to policy gridlock. But do a large fraction of legislators reject compromises, even when the compromise moves policy toward their preferred outcome? The results from the survey of state legislators presented in Chapter 2 show that nearly a quarter of state legislators say they would reject a proposal that moves the gas tax toward their preferred outcome. Legislators' rejection of half-loaf compromises exacerbates the difficulties of solving problems in a political environment polarized along ideological lines.

Why, then, do legislators sometimes reject the compromise that seems within reach and is closer to their preferred policy? Chapter 3 presents evidence that the belief that they will face a lot of punishment from their voters for compromising reduces legislators' likelihood of voting for a given compromise proposal by 21 percentage points. We find a similar effect among local elected officials. This demonstrates the importance of legislators' views of their constituents and the role that fear of voter punishment plays in the rejection of compromises. This finding also motivates the chapters that follow.

Chapter 4 explores which voters – general election voters, primary voters, or campaign donors – legislators fear will punish them for compromise. In-person surveys of state legislators confirm that legislators mostly fear punishment from primary voters. Legislators believe that primary voters prefer that legislators vote to kill compromise bills, worry that these primary voters will punish them if they support such legislation, and act in response to this concern. Beyond the patterns in surveys of state legislators, congressional roll call votes from 2011 to 2015 show that greater Tea Party support in a district predicted an increased likelihood that Republican House members voted against compromise bills. Together, these results highlight how legislators' concerns about how primary voters respond to compromise can dissuade legislators from compromising.

Chapter 5 shifts to focus on the public and whether legislators are accurate in their belief that primary voters are likely to punish them for compromising. An experimental survey vignette presented to a national sample of the public that matches a vignette used for legislators shows how people respond to their Senator's vote on a half-loaf compromise. Results suggest that most voters, whether or not they generally vote in primary elections, reward legislators for making compromises. At first blush this suggests that legislators may overestimate the punishment they would face from primary voters. However, the subset of co-partisan primary voters who oppose compromise on a specific issue *are* willing to punish legislators who vote for the compromise. Although legislators may benefit electorally from supporting compromise, especially in the general election, they have reason to be cautious on compromise bills to avoid voter backlash from small subsets of the politically active primary electorate.

Just because the subset of voters who punish legislators for compromising is small does not mean it cannot be consequential – a small subset can mobilize a strong challenger, paint a legislator's behavior as problematic in the eyes of less informed voters, or vote on the basis of a single important issue. Moreover, across many compromise votes a legislator may face, the small groups of voters who oppose each compromise might, when added together, represent a decisive portion of the primary electorate.

Given legislators' failure to support compromise proposals that break legislative gridlock, are there ways to alter the institutions and norms surrounding negotiation that might facilitate more compromise? Chapter 6 explores different approaches to negotiation with in-person survey experiments at the National Conference of State Legislatures Legislative Summit. In one of those experiments, legislators indicate that they are more likely to achieve compromise by negotiating in private (even as they express some trepidation about meeting in private). This suggests that private negotiations might make compromise easier to achieve.

Given the findings that legislators exacerbate gridlock by rejecting half-loaf compromises out of fear that they will be punished in primary elections, Chapter 7 discusses how to balance representation and accountability with processes that might better insulate legislators from their electoral fear as they seek to negotiate compromises. Ensuring that the public is knowledgeable about elected officials' decisions is an important facet of democratic accountability. Yet the watchful eye of primary voters may also deter legislators from considering reasonable compromises. Chapter 7 discusses how to balance these two considerations. It also discusses the role of communication. Our findings, as well as the comments from state legislators at the 2017 NCSL, emphasize the importance of communication between legislators and their constituents – explaining the legislative process, justifying choices, and developing a home style that cultivates trust (Fenno 1978). With greater communication and building of trust, legislators may have leeway to insulate portions of the legislative process from public scrutiny, helping them reach compromises and overcome gridlock.

2

Legislators Reject Half-Loaf Compromises

They want a "total solution" and let the perfect be the enemy of the good.
2017 NCSL Attendee 1

A reporter asked President Ronald Reagan how to describe his approach to governing during the 1980 primary election. He answered, "If I found when I was governor [of California] that I could not get 100 percent of what I asked for, I took 80 percent" (interview with Ronald Reagan, 1980). He contrasted his acceptance of compromise with others who "think that you should, on principle, jump off the cliff with the flag flying if you can't get everything you want" (interview with Ronald Reagan, 1980). Some state legislators we surveyed at the National Conference of State Legislatures (NCSL) in 2017 expressed a sentiment similar to Reagan's view: "½ way is better than nothing" (NCSL Attendee 8) and "½ of loaf better than no loaf" (NCSL Attendee 79). Recall that we define "half-loaf" compromises as any proposals that move policy closer to – but not all the way to – the legislator's preferred outcome.

The case of the San Rafael Swell illustrated that, if many legislators reject compromises, legislation may die even when the proposal represents a policy gain for a majority of those very legislators. Those who wanted more conservation amended the bill to bring the policy closer to what they wanted, which led to the death of the bill when the sponsor pulled it from consideration. In another instance, Democratic members of the 2011 deficit reduction "Super Committee" rejected a proposal initially heralded as a "breakthrough" by Senator Dick Durbin (D-IL). The proposal offered to raise revenues by $250 billion over ten years – including increased revenue from the top two tax brackets,

thereby making the tax code more progressive – as part of a broader plan
to rein in entitlement spending and reform the tax code (McCormack,
2011). Senator Pat Toomey (R-PA), who had proposed the compromise, complained that although "several of our Democratic colleagues
had repeatedly spoken about the virtues of tax simplification and
tax reform, they couldn't budge from the idea of a trillion dollar tax
increase" (McCormack 2011). In other words, he attributed the failure
of the legislation to Democratic legislators rejecting a compromise that
raised taxes – as the Democrats wanted – but raised those taxes by less
than those legislators would have preferred.

These stories challenge simple explanations of legislators' roll call
behavior. Just as we expect constituents to vote for the candidate whose
position on issues is closer to their preferred policies (Downs 1957), the
dominant models of policymaking predict that legislators vote for proposals that are closer to their preferred policy than the existing policy. Yet
policymakers appear to sometimes reject proposals that move policy in
the direction they want but fail to give them their most preferred outcome.

While the examples are suggestive, the complexity of policymaking in
a legislature hampers the evaluation of whether legislators systematically
reject half-loaf compromises. Not all examples are as straightforward as
the San Rafael Swell bill failure. We may not have good estimates of legislators' most preferred policy, the proposal, and the current policy. Moreover,
examples alone do not give a sense of how many legislators reject compromise. If such behavior is relatively rare, then it is not likely to be a major
roadblock to passing needed policies. But if it is relatively common, then it
may be an important explanation for legislative inaction. In this chapter,
we discuss half-loaf compromises in the context of the spatial model framework and present survey results that assess what fraction of legislators
reject offers that clearly move legislation closer to their ideal policy.

MODELS OF SPATIAL VOTING AND COMPROMISE PROPOSALS

Observers interested in trying to predict which legislators will support a
new proposal, and therefore whether it will pass, often start by looking at
how the new bill changes the status quo. For example, when the Waxman-
Markey cap and trade legislation (H.R. 2454 – the American Clean
Energy and Security Act)[1] passed the House and was being considered by

---

[1] This bill is known as Waxman-Markey after its authors Henry Waxman (D-CA) and
  Edward Markey (D-MA).

the Senate in 2009 and 2010, the *E&E Daily* produced lists of senators likely to be in favor of or opposed to the bill (E&E Daily, 2010). Because the bill moved policy in a liberal direction, thirty-seven legislators known to be liberal were expected to vote yes. Thirty-two known to be conservative were expected to vote no. That left thirty-one senators in the middle, whose position on the legislation would depend on the exact compromises made during the negotiation. The bill was never considered in the Senate, so we have no way to test whether the lists correctly identified the senators likely to support or oppose it. However, these lists exemplify the understanding that legislators are expected to vote on a proposal based on how close it is to their own ideological position.

Consistent with this perspective, spatial models with proximity voting predict that legislators and other key actors will accept proposals that are closer to their ideal point than the status quo (Brady and Volden 1998; Krehbiel 1998; Tsebelis 2002; Crisp et al. 2011; Bertelli and Grose 2006). These models assume that officials are rational actors who make decisions to maximize their policy preferences (Enelow and Hinich 1984). If a proposal is closer to the preferences of enough legislators, the policy should pass.

Figure 2.1 indicates the ideal policy for two different legislators (Leg A and Leg B) in a unidimensional policy space that goes from liberal to conservative. In this case, both legislators would prefer a policy that is more liberal than the status quo. These ideal policies represent legislators' induced preferences, which incorporate the preferences of their voters,

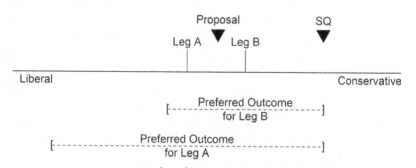

FIGURE 2.1. Preferred outcomes in a spatial model.
Note: The line represents a unidimensional policy space. Leg A and Leg B represent the ideal points of Legislator A and Legislator B. The triangle labeled Proposal represents a policy proposal and the triangle labeled SQ represents the status quo. Finally, the region where each legislator should prefer a proposal to the status quo is marked below by lines ending in brackets.

their party, and their own ideology (Levitt 1996).[2] A simple model of proximity voting would predict that each legislator would vote for a wide range of policies that are nearer to her ideal position than the status quo. This range of policies is symmetric around a legislator's preferred policy, defined by the status quo (SQ) on one side and an equivalent distance between the legislator's ideal point and the status quo on the other side.[3] This is marked in Figure 2.1 by lines ending in brackets. The standard uni-dimensional spatial model with proximity voting provides an unequivo-cal prediction of how frequently legislators should reject proposals in this region: never.

Consider immigration policy for undocumented immigrants brought to the United States by their parents (known as DREAMers after failed legislation to offer a process for citizenship). When the Trump Administration announced the end of new applications and an expira-tion of the Deferred Action for Childhood Arrivals (DACA) program – allowing immigrants brought to the country as minors to stay in the country legally – that revised policy became the status quo. SQ in Figure 2.1 represents this policy – what happens if no new bill is passed. However, President Trump requested that Congress take action regard-ing DACA, suggesting that there might be several means for changing policy. Suppose that legislators A and B would both prefer a less restric-tive position on the immigration status of DREAMers. Each would be expected to accept a wide range of policies corresponding to their pre-ferred outcomes as shown in Figure 2.1. Legislator B would accept poli-cies somewhat less restrictive than the status quo – perhaps an extension of the DACA program. Legislator A would accept an even larger range of policies, perhaps even extending toward the left (or liberal direction) to a path for citizenship for DREAMers. If the proposal in the figure came up, the standard unidimensional spatial model with proximity voting would predict that both legislators would vote for the proposal.

These models also provide a compelling explanation for why it is dif-ficult to move policy away from the status quo: if one or more pivotal actors with veto power prefer the status quo over the proposed alterna-tive, any policy change will be blocked (Brady and Volden 1998; Krehbiel 1998; Tsebelis 2002). These veto players can be the sixtieth senator whose vote is needed to end a filibuster, the median voter, the president,

---

[2] In preference-based accounts of legislator behavior, legislators are often viewed as aligning with the preferences of their voters, either through selection or electorally conscious constraints (Miller and Stokes, 1963).

[3] This can be written formally as SQ − 2 * | SQ − Legislator's Position |.

the legislators whose votes are needed to override a president's veto, or party/committee leaders who can keep the bill from getting to a vote (Carson et al. 2011b). If a key veto player prefers the status quo to the proposal, then the models would predict no change in policy. The narrative of polarization (McCarty et al. 2006; Theriault 2008; Mann and Ornstein 2012) emphasizes the role that widening ideological differences between pivotal legislators plays in limiting agreement.[4] Because the key actors do not share any common ground, proposals fail, preserving the status quo (Krehbiel 1998; Brady and Volden 1998). Voters too see polarization as a major obstacle to policymaking. A 2013 survey from Pew Research Center asked: "What's the main reason Congress can't get things done?" Forty-eight percent of Americans attributed inaction to the "parties having grown so far apart that they can't agree on solutions" (Pew Research Center, 2013). Gridlock may thus simply reflect the lack of common ground among the key actors involved in the process.

While polarization has certainly grown in the last several decades (McCarty et al., 2006) and is an important driver of gridlock in contemporary politics, ideological differences may not be the only reason for a lack of progress in solving the many problems that governments face. Gridlock may also occur because some legislators vote no, despite being faced with a policy proposal that is closer to their most preferred policy than the status quo. Some legislators recognize this behavior. When we asked state legislators at the 2017 NCSL why legislators reject compromises, one attendee told us: "Because it does not go far enough" (NCSL Attendee 183).

In short, legislators may reject compromises that the spatial model with proximity voting would suggest they should accept. When Representative Nancy Pelosi (D-CA) gave a speech regarding President Trump's termination of DACA and congressional efforts to make a deal to continue the program, she was greeted by protesters who sought action on not just the 800,000 DACA recipients, but on comprehensive immigration reform that might create paths for citizenship. As she put it, "This group today is saying don't do the Dream Act unless you do comprehensive immigration reform. Well, we all want to do comprehensive immigration reform...I understand their frustration – I'm excited by it as a matter of fact – but the fact is, they're completely wrong" (Sernoffsky, 2017). Pelosi believed a compromise on DACA would be

---

[4] While some work has pointed to strategy and competition as limiting agreement (Lee 2009, 2016; Harbridge 2015), a lack of common ground remains the prominent explanation for gridlock.

better than the status quo. Yet, a group of protesters from her district opposed the compromise because they wanted a larger change in immigration policy. They wanted her to reject a half-loaf offer in favor of hypothetical comprehensive reform even though she deemed comprehensive reform politically infeasible at that time. Thus, although we would expect Representative Pelosi to favor a compromise even if it did not achieve comprehensive reform, she might vote against it due to pressure from constituents. This chapter seeks to understand how likely legislators are to reject half-loaf compromises, while subsequent chapters disentangle why they oppose them.

For this study, we focus on cases of half-loaf compromises. For the individual legislator, which is the unit of analysis at which we study this phenomenon throughout the book, a half-loaf compromise (or half-loaf offer) is a proposal that is somewhere between her ideal policy and the status quo. The expression "half a loaf is better than none" is not restricted to cases where a legislator gets exactly half of what she wants, but rather is used broadly to mean getting only a portion of what she wants. Similarly, a half-loaf offer or compromise in this book does not have to be the midpoint between what the legislator wants and the status quo, though it can be. Rather, half-loaf offers are proposals that would give legislators some – but not all – of what they wanted.

The proposal in Figure 2.1 is just such a compromise for Legislator A. It moves policy toward her preferred outcome but not all the way. The spatial voting model of policymaking makes a clear prediction about these half-loaf compromises: policymakers should vote to pass them. In Figure 2.1, Legislator B finds the proposal more satisfactory, compared to the status quo; however, the proposal moves policy to the other side of Legislator B's preferred position, which could cause him to vote against the proposal if he cares primarily about whether policy falls to his left or his right (i.e., if he engages in directional voting). Instead, we focus only on compromises that move policy toward an individual's most preferred outcome but not toward the other side. The spatial model of voting makes the clear prediction that legislators should vote for these half-loaf compromises. Figure 2.2 illustrates the range of compromise proposals referred to as half-loaf offers in this book.

This specificity about our use of the term half-loaf compromise is in contrast to the varied ways that practitioners, pundits, and academics refer to compromise. They sometimes suggest compromise is simply consensus, as we see in Representative Ann McLane Kuster's

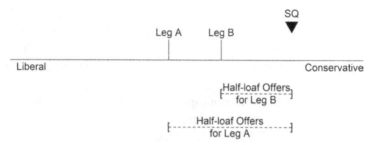

FIGURE 2.2. Examples of the range for half-loaf offers.

(D-NH) press release, in which she "praised her fellow freshman colleagues on both sides of the aisle for their early efforts to find common
ground, noting that meaningfully addressing our fiscal challenges will
require both parties to compromise" (Kuster 2013). At other times,
however, people refer to compromise as meeting in the middle, as with
Senate Appropriations Committee Chairman Daniel Inouye's (D-HI)
comments about funding bills divided between president's Obama's
request and what the House wanted: "The Senate has put forward a
reasonable, fiscally responsible bill that will reduce funding at a rate
that is $51 billion below the President's budget request.... This bill
is a good faith effort to meet in the middle" (Wildlife Management
Institute 2011; for other examples of meet-in-the-middle compromises, see Harbridge et al. 2014, Study 1; Wolak 2013, Study 1; Ryan
2017, Study 2). Sometimes, politicians talk about compromise when
one party capitulates to the demands of the other (Westwood 2014),
as when Republican Senate candidate Richard Mourdock (R-IN)
said, "I have a mindset that says bipartisanship ought to consist of
Democrats coming to the Republican point of view" (Zapler 2012).
Complicating the varied use of compromise further is how partisanship may alter which definition a legislative actor prefers. For some,
whether compromise entails meeting in the middle or one side capitulating depends upon which party is seeking the compromise. As one
Republican attendee at the NCSL told us: "Democrats think compromise is we go all the way to their side. Republicans think compromise
is we meet in the middle" (NCSL Attendee 252). Still others concep-
tualize compromise as balancing multiple interests and leaving none
fully satisfied (Glaser 2006). Finally, some scholars leave the definition of compromise unexplained (Maoz 2012; Ryan 2017, Study 1),
referring to it only in the abstract.

Employing a clear operationalization clarifies the conditions needed to identify half-loaf offers. The unequivocal prediction from the spatial model that legislators should accept all proposals that make them better off relative to the status quo relies on a few assumptions. First, it relies on the assumption that the policy space is unidimensional – that a single issue or ideological dimension can capture policy locations, preferences, and the status quo. For most of US history, one dimension ranging from liberal to conservative has explained most of the variation in voting behavior in Congress. But there has often been a second dimension corresponding to civil rights issues (Poole and Rosenthal 1997) and in many specific policy areas, legislation can be multidimensional (Jochim and Jones 2013). In surveying legislators about half-loaf offers, we focus on the unidimensional case where we can avoid concerns about estimating how each legislator weighs the importance of the two dimensions.[5]

Second, the spatial voting model's prediction assumes legislators have single-peaked preferences. That is, the model assumes that each legislator has one ideal point in the policy dimension and that policies further from that ideal point are less preferred. Most scholars are fairly confident in this assumption about political elites, even as the public shows less ideological constraint (Converse 1964) and evidence of double-peaked preferences (Egan 2014). Like other scholars, we assume politicians have single-peaked preferences.

Third, the spatial model assumes preferences represent the position of the legislator, accounting for their personal preference as well as those of their constituents and other actors (Fiorina 1974; Ramey 2015; Shapiro et al. 1990). This is often referred to as the legislator's induced preference. We went to great lengths to elicit legislators' induced preferences about the issue at hand, asking them about their own preferences, the preferences of their constituents, and the preferences of their party leaders before asking for their induced preferences. This operationalization of preferences aims to encourage legislators to report their induced preference in their official capacity in keeping with the assumptions of the spatial model.

Fourth, users of the spatial voting model often assume sincere behavior – what we would expect from legislators if this is a one-shot effort at policy change. In a single round of bargaining, a rational

---

[5] In some circumstances, it can be difficult to limit the policy space to one dimension. As a result, some specifications in later chapters of this book invoke a second dimension. In this chapter, where we estimate the prevalence of half-loaf compromise rejections, we presented situations to legislators that represent only one dimension.

legislator should accept any proposal that in her view improves on the status quo. When we asked legislators about half-loaf offers, our language indicated that the offered proposal was a take-it or leave-it opportunity, not the initial salvo in multiple rounds of bargaining (e.g., Cameron 2000; Kousser and Phillips 2009). This allows us to focus on those policy compromises where the predictions from the spatial model are clearest. Under these four standard assumptions, our definition of half-loaf compromise allows us to look at cases in which we can cleanly test whether legislators reject compromises that the spatial model predicts they should accept.

Finally, the specificity of the definition of half-loaf compromise makes it easier to be consistent when studying or discussing compromises across different levels of government. Many of the examples presented so far illustrate failures of half-loaf compromises at the federal level, but there is no reason to think it is confined to the federal level. Decision-makers at all levels of government are faced with the same basic decision framework. At the federal, state, and local level, each proposal is set against existing policy (or lack of policy). And each elected official must decide whether to support the proposal or reject it in favor of the status quo. In the remainder of the book, we study state legislators, city officials, members of Congress, and the public to understand how frequently politicians reject half-loaf offers and why they do so.

In order to quantify the degree to which rejection of compromise occurs (even in the simplest cases of unidimensional policies and one-shot offers) we presented state legislators with a simple policy proposal that is halfway between their ideal policy and the status quo – a proposal that the simple spatial model unequivocally predicts the legislator should accept. If the legislator votes against the proposal, she is voting against a proposal that is closer to her ideal point than the status quo policy. The use of a midway proposal eliminates concerns that legislators might vote against a policy because they engage in directional voting (Rabinowitz and Macdonald 2014).

The rejection of half-loaf compromises is puzzling both intuitively – as the offered compromise is closer to the legislator's preferred policy – and in light of the more formal theoretical predictions of the spatial model. The emphasis on half-loaf offers keeps a spotlight on the unexpected behavior of rejecting compromise legislation even when it gives legislators part of what they want. The rest of this chapter presents two studies that use online surveys to determine how often state legislators and city officials reject these compromise proposals.

STATE LEGISLATORS AND COMPROMISE ON THE GAS TAX

In 2014, we surveyed state legislators throughout the United States to determine how they would respond to a half-loaf offer to change their state's gas tax. We emailed all state legislators who had publicly listed an email address on their state's legislative website to invite them to take a short survey on "how state legislators make policy decisions." The email was sent from the university account of one of the researchers. In addition to the initial invitation, we sent two follow up invitations; each follow up invitation came a week after the prior email was sent.

The invitations yielded a sample size of 257 state legislators. The sample is restricted to the legislators who had an ideal policy different from the current gas tax in their state.[6] This represents a response rate of about 5%,[7] within the range of response rates reported in the literature[8] and consistent with the pattern of declining response rates for surveys of political elites (Butler and Powell 2014; Fisher and Herrick 2013; Maestas et al. 2003). To ensure that the low response rate does not bias the results, we evaluate the representativeness of the sample and faithfully follow the pre-analysis plan to avoid data mining.

Overall, the sample was fairly balanced relative to the national composition of state legislators based upon gender, majority/minority status, and term-limited or not. For instance, women represented 28% of the state sample compared to 24% nationally (National Conference of State Legislatures, 2013) and 27% of the sample came from states with term-limits compared to 26% nationally (Ballotpedia 2014c). The sample skewed slightly Democratic; 43% of the survey respondents were Republicans compared to

---

[6] The first question on the survey asked: "Before we start, are you a legislator or staff member?" Overall there were about 350 responses, but as indicated in our pre-analysis plan filed with the Experiments in Governance and Politics (EGAP) network we limited our analysis to the sample to self-identified legislators. Only responses from state legislators are included in the percentages rejecting compromise reported here. It is possible that some state staff answered the survey on behalf of a legislator *and* reported being the legislator. Even if that occurred, it is unlikely to have changed the result because in the other studies we did where we know who filled out the survey – because it was done face-to-face at the National Conference of State Legislatures, e.g., see Chapter 6 – the results do not differ when staff are included in the analysis.

[7] The low response rate is likely a manifestation of the tragedy of the commons. With the ability to easily contact state legislators via email, many more people (both scholars and others) are now conducting national surveys than they have in previous years. Many legislators told us that they were turning us down because they received too many of these requests.

[8] In surveys of the public, telephone response rates range from 4 to 70% (Holbrook et al. 2008) and web survey response rates are even lower (e.g., Sax et al. 2003).

TABLE 2.1. *Comparison of state legislator survey sample to state legislator population*

Attribute	Percent in Sample	Percent in Population
Female	28	24
Republican	43	52*
Term Limits	27	26
In Majority	63	64

	Mean in Sample	Mean in Population
Squire Index	0.17	0.20*

* A chi-squared test indicates that the party distribution in the sample is significantly different (at $p < 0.05$) than the distribution in the population, or a *t*-test, indicates that the mean for the sample Squire Index is significantly different from the mean in the population (at $p < 0.05$, two-sided). For all other attributes, we reject the null that the distributions are different (or that the mean in the sample is different from the mean in the population). The Squire Index measures the degree of professionalism across legislatures.

52% nationally (Ballotpedia 2014a, 2014b). This is similar to other studies surveying state legislators (Harden 2013; Broockman and Skovron 2018; Butler et al. 2017). And the sample mean for professionalism, as measured by the Squire Index (Squire 2007), is slightly lower than the mean for the population of state legislators. Table 2.1 compares the sample to national numbers for each of the characteristics discussed above, showing that partisanship and professionalism are the only two characteristics where the differences between the sample and population are statistically significant. Further, we have broad representation even for these variables. The sample's relatively high degree of representativeness across the characteristics increases confidence in the generalizability of the findings.

The need to identify legislators' preferences and the location of current policy in the same dimension is central to the application of spatial models in politics (Krehbiel and Rivers 1988; see also Adams et al. 2011; Jessee 2009, 2012; Joesten and Stone 2014; Stone and Simas 2010; Volden 1998). Although there are many instances in which it appears that policymakers reject compromises, cases reported in the press are often indeterminate because we do not have information about all possible inputs for these legislators' decisions. Measuring the specific values of all the major elements in a voting decision – the status quo, the legislator's preference, and the location of the proposal – on the same scale (Krehbiel and Rivers 1988) is a major obstacle to studying how legislators deal with compromise proposals.

Focusing on the gas tax solves these measurement problems by identifying the precise values of the elements that go into analyzing whether
legislators act in a way that is consistent with spatial voting. Unlike more
abstract policies (such as the degree to which a policy is pro-choice versus pro-life), legislators have a shared understanding of what a given
change in the gas tax represents because the gas tax can be expressed
in the simple, unidimensional terms of cents per gallon. We thus locate
legislators' preferences (acquired from the survey), the status quo (taken
from state law), and the policy proposal under consideration (given in
the vignette presented to legislators as shown in Figure 2.3). Importantly,
this means that legislators were presented with a half-loaf offer that they
should strictly prefer based upon their preferences and the status quo.

The gas tax was a salient issue for state officials and many of their
constituents in 2014 when we surveyed them (Schaper 2014). The NCSL
includes gas tax legislation as part of the searchable database for state
legislators (National Conference of State Legislatures 2014) and the
database reports that twenty-six states considered sixty-nine bills that
in some way dealt with state gas taxes in 2014 – the year of our survey. Moreover, nine state legislators at the NCSL in 2017 volunteered
anecdotes associated with a gas tax vote when asked in an open-ended
question for an example of an issue where legislators who supported a
compromise faced voter punishment.[9]

The first step to identifying whether legislators reject a compromise
that explicitly moves policy toward their ideal outcome is to measure
legislators' policy preferences. The survey led up to a question on legislators' ideal policy by reminding them of their state's current gas tax
level and then asking them about the preferences of three key sets of
actors (Levitt, 1996): (1) the voters in their district; (2) their legislative
party leaders; and (3) themselves. Asking about the position of voters,
legislative party leaders, and themselves primed them to think about the
various factors that shape the position they ultimately report as their
preferred policy, or their induced preference. We reminded legislators
about their state's current gas tax because legislators have information
about the status quo when making decisions.

---

[9] Here are a few examples of what they wrote:
"We have a recall for a Senator for voting for a gas bill" (2017 NCSL Attendee 88).
"Tax hike for transportation in VA. Much R party retribution for compromise" (2017 NCSL Attendee 20).
"Look at gas tax votes across the country – I think 80% of those who voted for the gas tax have been primaried in the Republican Party" (2017 NCSL Attendee 252).

Sometimes state gas taxes are proposed as a way to encourage fuel conservation and reduce carbon emissions (in addition to being a source of funding). Currently the gas tax in Arkansas is about 22 cents per gallon.

We want to ask you about the following three groups' preferences over the optimal state gas tax level.

[Note: As you answer these questions, be sure that the number you've selected appears on the right side of the slider. If a number does not appear on the right, you have not yet answered this question. If the answer is more than 150 cents/gallon, enter 150 here and we'll give you a chance to enter the larger number.]

0 15 30 45 60 75 90 105 120 135 150

The preferred level for **voters** in your district	
The preferred level of your legislative **party leaders**	
Your preferred level	

We realize that many factors go into making decisions as a state legislator. Accounting for all of the above considerations (and other factors too), what would you implement if, in your role as a state legislator, you could choose the state gas tax level in your state?

[Note: As you answer these questions, be sure that the number you've selected appears on the right side of the slider. If a number does not appear on the right, you have not yet answered this question. If the answer is more than 150 cents/gallon, enter 150 here and we'll give you a chance to enter the larger number.]

0 15 30 45 60 75 90 105 120 135 150

| Your chosen level as a state legislator | |

FIGURE 2.3. Survey to assess gas tax preferences used for Arkansas legislator.

Legislators indicated their perceptions about the preferences of each group of actors for state gas tax levels on a scale that ranged from zero to $1.50 per gallon (state gas taxes in 2014 ranged from eight to fifty cents per gallon).[10] Then they answered the following question designed to identify their preferred policy: "We realize that many factors go into

[10] One hundred fifty cents per gallon is higher than the optimal gas taxes given by economists (Lin and Prince 2009; Parry and Small 2005). However, respondents were allowed to enter an even higher number to leave room for those who wanted to dramatically increase the gas tax. Less than 1%, two legislators, chose to enter a higher number back in period. Those who did enter a higher cost were treated in the analysis as having chosen $1.50 per gallon. Excluding them from the analysis had no effect on the result.

making decisions as a state legislator. Accounting for all of the above considerations (and other factors too), what would you implement if, in your role as a state legislator, you could choose the state gas tax level in your state?" The question emphasized that they should think about their role as a state legislator to capture how they would act in their official capacity. Rather than report their personal position, the question was designed to elicit the preferred position they would use to make decisions (i.e., their induced preference). The word "implement" was used to elicit their preferred policy as opposed to what they thought was politically viable. Figure 2.3 shows the exact wording of these questions.

One advantage of surveying state legislators on the gas tax is the ability to validate the survey responses by comparing their self-reported preferences with the actual voting record. Among the states that considered the gas tax in 2014, two states (New Hampshire and Wyoming) had recorded roll call votes on bills that focused primarily on the gas tax and while meeting two other criteria: (1) that there were enough survey respondents from these states to conduct a statistical analysis of their voting; and (2) that voting did not break down only along party lines. We use legislators' reports of their preferred policy as a predictor of their votes in the respective states (for more details, see Anderson et al. 2016).[11] In 2014, New Hampshire's Senate Bill 367 raised the gas tax from eighteen to twenty-two and two-tenth cents per gallon. Though support for the bill was split, the bill passed by a fifteen to nine margin in the New Hampshire State Senate and a 193–141 margin in the New Hampshire State House.[12] In 2013, the Wyoming legislature considered House Bill 69, which raised the gas tax from fourteen to twenty-four cents per gallon. In Wyoming, the State Senate passed the measure by a margin of eighteen to twelve and the Wyoming State House passed it by a margin of thirty-five to twenty-four.[13]

To validate the survey measures, we tested whether legislators' reported preferences predict their roll call votes. The dependent variable is an indicator variable that takes a value of one when legislators voted for the bill to increase the gas tax and zero when they voted against the bill. We regress legislators' roll call votes on their *preferences for*

---

[11] Table 2.2 and accompanying text (lightly edited) appears in our *Legislative Studies Quarterly* article (Anderson et al. 2016).

[12] More information about the bill can be found at http://openstates.org/nh/bills/2014/SB367/.

[13] More information about the bill can be found at http://openstates.org/wy/bills/2013/HB69/.

TABLE 2.2. *Predicting legislators' roll call votes using their reported ideal policies*

Dependent Variable = Vote to Increase Gas Tax	(1)	(2)
Preference for Proposal over Status Quo	0.047*	0.033*
| SQ – Ideal | – | Proposal – Ideal |	(0.011)	(0.010)
Republican		−0.48*
		(0.10)
Intercept	0.45*	0.73*
	(0.064)	(0.081)
N	58	58
R-Squared	0.25	0.46

Note: The data come from the votes on Wyoming House Bill 69 (in 2013) and New Hampshire Senate Bill 367 (in 2014). The dependent variable is an indicator that takes a value of one when the legislator voted to increase the gas tax and zero when they voted against the gas tax increase. Both models estimated using OLS regressions. Standard errors are in parentheses.
* $p < 0.05$ (one-sided).

the proposal over the status quo, operationalized by taking the absolute difference between the status quo and their ideal policy minus the absolute difference of the proposal and their ideal policy (i.e., | SQ – Ideal | – | Proposal – Ideal |). This measure takes a positive/negative value when the proposal/status quo is closer to the legislator's preference. Thus, a statistically significant, positive coefficient would be evidence that legislators' ideal policies (as reported in the survey) are predictors of their roll call votes.

Table 2.2 displays linear probability models, with Column (1) presenting the results of a bivariate relationship and Column (2) presenting the results controlling for partisanship. Legislators' induced preferences, as reported in the survey, predict roll call votes, and the effect remains strong and statistically significant, even when controlling for the legislators' partisanship. The evidence shows that legislators' self-reported preferences are a good predictor of how they actually voted on gas tax legislation. Substantively, the effect is meaningful. For example, if the gas tax proposal was between the legislator's ideal point and the status quo, moving the policy just a half-cent closer to the legislator's preference (and thus also a half-cent away from the status quo) would result in a 3.3 percentage point increase in the likelihood that a legislator would vote for the bill. For larger changes in the proposal – such as the magnitudes seen in the New Hampshire and Wyoming bills – the change in the likeli-hood of voting for the bill is substantial. These self-reported preferences are not cheap talk; the measure of the legislators' preferred outcome, indicated in their responses, can be externally validated. This suggests, reassuringly, that our analysis can provide insights into how legislators respond to policy proposals they consider while in office.

The survey then presented legislators with a proposal they might see in their legislature in order to learn how they would respond to it. Legislators were asked how they would vote on a compromise proposal to set the gas tax at a level halfway between the current policy and their most preferred policy. For instance, if a legislator from Arkansas, which had a state tax of twenty-two cents, stated that she would choose to implement a state gas tax of forty-four cents per gallon, the proposal would be thirty-three cents per gallon. The legislator was then asked, "Would you vote for this bill if it were introduced in your legislature?" The full text of the vignette is given in Figure 3.1 in Chapter 3, in which we discuss parts of the vignette that were randomized across legislators. Figure 2.4 illustrates the scenario that a legislator from Arkansas would face in the example above. As the figure shows, the proposal moves policy in the legislator's preferred direction. A legislator who wanted to decrease the gas tax was correspondingly given a half-loaf proposal that decreased the gas tax. According to the spatial model with proxim-ity voting, each legislator should strictly prefer this half-loaf offer and vote for it.

Despite the clear prediction that each legislator should vote for the proposal, many legislators say they would reject it: Figure 2.5 displays the results. Surprisingly, 23% of state legislators say they would vote

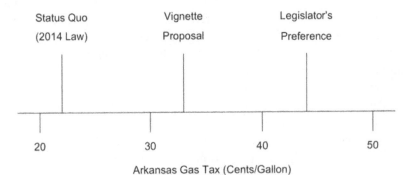

FIGURE 2.4. Hypothetical example for legislator from Arkansas.

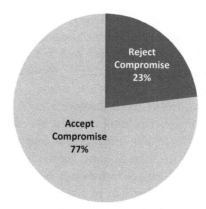

FIGURE 2.5. Many state legislators reject the half-loaf compromise.
Note: N = 257.

against the half-loaf compromise that would move the gas tax closer to their preferred outcome. Nearly a quarter of legislators reject a proposal that would make them better off on policy grounds.

CITY OFFICIALS AND COMPROMISE ON BUDGET PRIORITIES

A subsequent follow-up study with elected city officials shows that this pattern of legislators rejecting compromise generalizes across policy areas and among various elected officials. Survey responses from city officials provide another opportunity to observe how lawmakers respond to half-loaf compromise offers in a context that shares many characteristics with federal and state policymaking (Trounstine 2009). In the summer of 2016, we asked a large sample of city officials about their preferences for their city budget and whether they would accept a half-loaf compromise.

Individuals invited to take part in the survey were drawn from a list purchased from Know Who, an organization that collects contact information from webpages of officials serving in cities with over 10,000 people. The organization uses web crawler software to identify when contact information changes on an official's webpage: the organization then has research assistants update the contact list of officials accordingly. Invitations to participate in our survey were sent in May and June of 2016 to elected city officials (e.g., mayors, city councillors, aldermen, supervisors) in 4,187 cities. This approach had a fairly high error rate. Based on Qualtrics' email tracking, 18,567 (or 67%) of the email invitations were delivered to an active email address. In addition, a manual search of a sample of 832 officials in the list found that only 44% of the email addresses were accurate. Taking these deficiencies into account, the survey had a response rate between 11.7 and 17.8%.[14]

The final sample of 1,440 respondents included a mix of officials from both the Democrat and Republican parties, with 37% identifying as Republican, 36% identifying as Democrat, 25% identifying as independents, and 2% of the remaining respondents identifying as "other." As the partisan breakdown demonstrates, non-partisan officials are more common in local politics than in state legislatures. The officials were generally part of the majority coalitions in their cities, with 80% saying that they were on the winning side of formal votes "most of the time." This study tests whether the rejection of half-loaf compromise replicates across samples.

This second study has a few key differences from the first study of state legislators. The wording of the proposed compromise in the study of city officials more closely matches bargaining situations in which lawmakers might be pivotal because they face a divided governing body where about half of the officials have different preferences. Further, we vary two features of the vignette in this study to show that elected officials generally pursue their own policy interests. First, we vary how much they are forced to give up in the compromise; they should be less likely to support compromises where they have to give up more. Second, we assign some of the city officials to a policy area where their preferred policy matches the status quo; those who want to keep the status quo should be more likely to reject a compromise than those who want to change the status quo.

In the survey, city officials selected one area of the budget they thought should get a greater share of the budget than it does now, one area that should receive a smaller share of the budget, and one area of the budget that should remain the same. The budget areas from which they could choose were education, public safety, the library, public works, parks and recreation, and street maintenance. City officials were then randomly questioned about one of the budget areas they selected and asked what percentage of the current budget allocation it should receive.[15]

---

[14] The survey was conducted in two waves sent to two different samples of city officials. The questions we analyze here were only included in the first wave of the survey to keep the survey from being too long.

[15] Because we could only randomize for those who provided preferences for a budget area to increase, to decrease, and to keep the same, 100 respondents who only answered one or two of the three questions were dropped from the sample, resulting in the final sample of 1,440 respondents.

If the city official was randomly assigned to an area where she indicated a preference for changing the share of the budget, she also reported the percentage of the budget she thought should be spent on that area. The official was then told that roughly half of the officials agreed with her stance and half wanted to keep spending at last year's level, and she was offered a compromise between her preferred spending change and the current level of spending – a half-loaf compromise. For example, if a city official wanted to change public safety spending from 15% of the budget to 25% of the budget, she was offered the following vignette:

Imagine that you were in negotiations where roughly half of the city officials want to keep the level of spending on public safety the same but you and the others want to increase spending on public safety by 10 percentage points so that it represents 25 percent of the budget, as you told us in the last set of questions. If there was a proposal to increase spending on public safety by 5 percentage points so that it represented 20 percent of the city's budget, how would you vote?

This example closely matches the halfway compromise offered to the state legislators. In this study, however, we also randomized whether officials were offered a proposal halfway between their preferred level and the status quo or somewhere along a continuum between the two endpoints; for officials who preferred the status quo, the proposal was between the status quo and the randomly assigned stance of the opposing side. Instead of being offered a compromise of an increase of five percentage points given the increase of ten percentage points that the official wanted, the city official might instead have been offered a compromise of an increase ranging from one percentage point to nine percentage points. Because the halfway bargain matches the state legislator study, we do not assign the bargains seen by respondents with equal probability. Instead, we place more city officials into the bargaining condition of receiving the halfway compromise and fewer into the more extreme compromises. The closeness of the offered compromise to the official's preferred change was randomly chosen; the choices and the associated probabilities are given in Table 2.3.

Among officials who wanted to change spending on an issue, nearly 13% still reject the compromise that moved policy part of the way to their preferred outcome (Figure 2.6). Those asked to concede more in the

TABLE 2.3. *Offers used in the city official survey vignette*

Closeness of offer	0.1	0.2	0.3	0.4	0.5	0.6	0.7	0.8	0.9
Probability	1/15	1/15	2/15	2/15	3/15	2/15	2/15	1/15	1/15

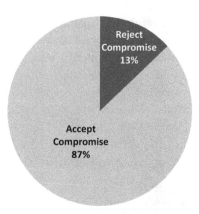

FIGURE 2.6. Many city officials reject compromise.
Note: The sample is limited to those who wanted to change spending on the issue. N = 972.

compromise were more likely to reject it, indicating that officials understood the bargaining situation and that achieving compromise can be more difficult when concessions in compromise proposals require some groups to give up more than others. For instance, 7.7% of those offered half of the change they sought rejected the compromise, and 19% of those offered only 20% of the change they sought rejected it.

To further evaluate whether city officials understood the logic of the hypothetical bargaining situation, some officials were randomly assigned to an area they indicated should remain the same. These officials were told that they were bargaining with others who wanted to change the allocation in that area. The percentage change that the opposition wanted was randomly assigned to be a five, ten, fifteen, or twenty percentage point increase or decrease. The city official was offered a compromise between that change and their preferred option of no change. Fifty-nine percent of these officials reject the compromise, as the spatial model predicts they should. When city officials who were assigned to an area where they did not want budgetary change are included along with those who wanted to change policy, 28% of the officials rejected the compromise proposal.

Comparing the two studies, city officials are less likely to reject the half-loaf offer than state legislators, perhaps because city politics is a less-politicized, low-information environment.[16] Still, more than one in eight officials who were assigned to a budget area where they wanted

---

[16] The difference in the rejection rates between the two samples is statistically significant ($p < 0.001$, two-sided). This substantive difference may relate to the nature of city officials' positions. For example, many cities hold nonpartisan races that do not have primaries.

to change spending rejected a policy that gave them part of what they wanted. The results from the second study of city officials are consistent with the first study of state legislators, providing further evidence that this is a widespread phenomenon.

DISCUSSION

Many elected officials, about a quarter of state legislators and about one in eight local officials, rejected the half-loaf compromise offered to them. The rejection is puzzling in light of predictions from the spatial model that suggest legislators should accept a half-loaf offer because it is closer to their preferred policy than the status quo.

Our findings suggest that reaching a compromise can be even more difficult than classic models of policymaking suggest. Compromise proposals that make majorities (or supermajorities if the institution requires them) better off on policy grounds are not sufficient to resolve gridlock. Though many instances of legislators' inability to find a suitable compromise reflect divergent views among the central players in the policymaking process that result from increasing ideological polarization, other instances may reflect lawmakers failing to support compromise proposals even if these compromises make them better off on policy grounds. This finding adds to a growing body of research on the strategic aspects of partisan conflict (Lee 2009, 2016; Harbridge 2015; Theriault 2015; Lebo et al. 2007; Koger and Lebo 2017) and isolates the role that rejection of half-loaf compromises plays in gridlock. Not only do conservatives and liberals want to move in opposite directions on many policies, but many legislators reject half-loaf offers that are closer to their own policy preferences. Although our finding that only

Perhaps they are less worried about punishment from voters who oppose compromise because they do not have to face primary voters. Also, most cities deal with less politicized issues that may be unlikely to mobilize voters who oppose compromise on these issues. If these factors are partially the cause of the difference in the rejection rates across the samples, then this finding is in line with what we would expect, given the results discussed in later chapters. However, the evidence here is at best tentative because the two groups of officials were asked different questions. We asked state legislators about the gas tax, but we asked city officials about various aspects of the city budget. Both of these questions deal with funding issues, but the gas tax seems to be a particularly salient issue for many voters because they see the impact of the policy on a regular basis at gas stations. Although this difference between the samples supports our other conclusions, we cannot rule out that this difference is simply due to a difference in survey questions. Whether and why rates of rejection of compromise differ across policy issues and across different electoral structures is an interesting question for future research.

a quarter of state legislators reject compromise may seem like a small fraction – as the majority of legislators do accept the compromise – such rejections can be consequential. Rather than simply moving policy to a position that garners the support of the median voter, a proposal would need to move policy toward a supermajority of legislators. This pattern highlights the need to understand why these compromise solutions fail; this understanding is crucial for developing remedies for gridlock. In Chapter 3 we test predictions about what increases legislators' likelihood of rejecting half-loaf offers.

3

Legislators Reject Half-Loaf Compromises Because They Fear Voter Retribution

> Fear of retribution is the primary reason preventing compromise.
>
> 2017 NCSL Attendee 142

A surprising number of legislators indicated that they would vote against proposals that move policy closer to their preferred policy. This behavior is puzzling because there are clear advantages for legislators who vote for half-loaf compromises. Most importantly, voting yes on these proposals makes legislators better off on policy grounds. So why would legislators vote against a half-loaf offer? One reason may be that there is a tension between their electoral interests and their policy interests.

This chapter explores several factors that may increase the likelihood that legislators would reject proposals that move policy closer to what they want. Reelection-minded legislators may fear voter retribution if they vote for a compromise, especially if they believe large numbers of voters decry compromise (Skocpol and Williamson 2012; Pew 2014b). Issues that are seen in moral terms make the public less likely to accept compromise (Mooney and Schuldt 2008), suggesting that electorally minded legislators may view compromises on issues framed in moral terms as unacceptable as well. Within the institutional arrangement of a competitive party system, there are also factors that may discourage legislators from supporting a compromise. A compromise that benefits the opposition party may have collective electoral costs for the party, as legislators may fear it will dilute the credit their party can claim for improving the policy (Lee 2016; Koger and Lebo 2017). In addition, a compromise that achieves partial policy benefits in the short term may make it harder to get a better policy in the future, which may discourage compromise if the legislator believes that she will be in a better position in the future to get all of what she wants (Volden 1998).[1]

The following section develops our theoretical expectations about the electoral and institutional factors that raise the costs of compromise and may therefore make a legislator more likely to reject a half-loaf compromise. Prior to fielding the survey of state legislators, we filed a pre-analysis plan (see Humphreys et al. 2013; Monogan 2013) with Evidence in Governance and Politics (EGAP) that detailed our hypotheses that legislators will be more likely to reject compromise if they (1) expect greater voter punishment for compromise; (2) see an argument framed in moral terms; (3) are presented a proposal sponsored by the opposition party; and/or (4) expect those who agree with them to increase in power in the future. We test these hypotheses following the proposal we specified in the pre-analysis plan.

The ideas underlying all four of these hypotheses are reflected in the anecdotal comments gathered from attendees at the National Conference of State Legislatures in 2017. In a pen and paper survey with a series of open-ended questions, we asked what led legislators to reject half-loaf compromises. Echoing the quote that opened this chapter, one attendee responded that it was driven by "fear of voter backlash and for ideological reasons" (2017 NCSL Attendee 11). This suggests that some legislators may perceive that voters oppose compromise and therefore legislators fear punishment if they support compromise. Another attendee pointed to the rationale surrounding the moral framing hypothesis, stating that, "Legislators reject compromise when they feel the issue relates to a core, moral principle" (2017 NCSL Attendee 31). Another member was quite blunt about how the partisanship of the bill's sponsor affects support for a compromise. "In my experience, I have seen Republicans vote against legislation if a Dem brings it" (2017 NCSL Attendee 175). Another attendee wrote that legislators would reject compromise, "If they believe holding out w/ a voting bloc could lead to a better outcome – i.e. not voting for a 1% corporate tax increase if they think they can hold out

---

[1] Pressure from party leaders is also likely part of the story. We opt not to focus on party pressure for two reasons. First, there are many forms of party pressure (direct and indirect) that may not be well captured in a vignette (or any other simplified version of policymaking that could be tractably studied via a survey). Second, pressure from party leaders to reject half-loaf compromises would simply raise the question of why leaders urge rejection of such compromise. We would still want to know why party leaders are against this proposal. Our approach is to focus on the underlying reasons legislators might oppose compromise.

and get 3%" (2017 NCSL Attendee 82). This suggests that the legislator believes that rejecting a compromise now could lead to a better outcome in the future. In sum, those working in state politics think that all of these factors might be related to legislators' rejection of compromise. Our goal in this chapter is to assess which factors, if any, *systematically* predict this behavior.

All four hypotheses are tested in the survey of state legislators about the gas tax and the two hypotheses on voter punishment and future power are also tested in the survey of city officials about local spending. These analyses show that fear of voter retribution for compromise is the key predictor of legislators' rejection of half-loaf offers. State legislators and city officials who believe that their voters are likely to punish them for compromising are significantly more likely to oppose the compromise proposal. We find no support for the other three explanations.

THE VOTER PUNISHMENT EXPLANATION

Legislators at both the national and subnational levels must try to be responsive to voters if they want to win reelection (Mayhew 1974; Fiorina 1983; Wolak 2017a). Although legislators might fear punishment for compromise from primary election voters, general election voters, voters who donate, or all of these voters, there are strong reasons to expect that the threat of punishment is more likely to come from voters in the primaries. Analyzing Pew data from 2014 (Pew 2014a) shows that while 61% of voters indicated they favor legislators who compromise, not all voters equally value compromise. Some constituents want bipartisanship and legislative compromise (Harbridge and Malhotra 2011); others, particularly strong partisans, do not (Harbridge et al. 2014). Less than half of very liberal and very conservative voters (46%) in the Pew poll said that they support legislators who compromise. Support was even lower when Tea Party supporters were isolated, with only 37% of Tea Party supporters saying that they support legislators who compromise. These voters' opposition to compromise is not limited to compromise in the abstract. For instance, in the 2011 budget debates, two-thirds of Republicans who identified with the Tea Party favored a government shutdown over compromise (Pew 2011).

If legislators believe that enough of their voters, perhaps especially their co-partisan voters (Fiorina 1974), are willing to punish them for compromising, they may be less likely to compromise. Voters can punish compromise in the primary election by supporting the legislator's opponent or in the general election by supporting the opposition candidate or by opting not to vote at all. Legislators who expect such punishment from their electorate, or even a small but key subset of voters, may reject compromises out of fear of this electoral retribution. This leads to our first hypothesis.

Voter Punishment Hypothesis: Legislators who fear electoral
retribution for compromise may reject compromise proposals.

The survey of state legislators enables us to assess legislators' beliefs about the likelihood that their voters will punish them for compromise, rather than relying on demographic attributes of the district. While there are reasons to think that this fear of punishment is likely to be focused on primary voters, we start by looking at a more general fear of voters. After exploring the role of voter punishment generally in this chapter, Chapter 4 delves more deeply into the electoral source of the fear of voter punishment and whether this is driven by concerns about the primary or general electorate.

THE MORAL FRAMING EXPLANATION

Some NCSL Summit attendees highlighted how moral understandings of an issue could reduce support for compromise. In their assessment of contemporary crises in American politics, Lane and Oreskes (2007, 7) concur, writing "the more the issue has a moral dimension, the more potentially awful the compromise can look." This suggests that the electoral costs of accepting a half-loaf compromise may be higher when the policy is framed as a moral issue. Indeed, political moralizing can reorient how individuals think about political disagreements. This is because it connects issues to deeply held beliefs about right and wrong (Lakoff 2002; Kahan and Braman 2006). When individuals think about an issue in moral terms, they turn from caring about what is most effective to focusing on adhering to what is right (Bennis et al. 2010; Ryan 2017) or to their core values (Kahan and Braman 2006). For example, a study of US adults shows that on issues such as gay marriage and abortion, the majority of respondents (55%) believe that people just need to apply their basic moral values to determine their policy position. By contrast, only about 25% of respondents feel that relying on basic moral values can resolve the conflict between civil liberties and security (Mooney and Schuldt 2008). In short, among the public, moralizing attitudes changes the types of positions and policies people are willing to accept (see Clifford and Jerit 2013; Feinberg and Willer 2013; Ryan 2014, 2017), making people less likely to compromise (Mooney and Schuldt 2008). These moralized attitudes resist change (e.g., Ritov and Baron 1999) and can even become entrenched when brought into the realm of policy and political tradeoffs (Ginges et al. 2007). As a result, new information about the effectiveness of a moralized policy is unlikely to change people's positions.

How issues are discussed, and whether this invokes moral considerations, may also matter. Rhetorical frames rooted in moral values lead audiences to interpret issues based on their underlying cultural values (Spielvogel 2005; Lakoff 2014). In 2018 and 2019, US legislators took to framing a fight over government funding for a border wall between the United States and Mexico in moral terms. Some commentators suggested this framing might make compromise harder to find. For example, Steve Inskeep of NPR's Morning Edition asked Representative Tom Suozzi (D-NY) how his party could possibly find common ground once Democratic Speaker Nancy Pelosi called the border wall an "immorality" (Inskeep 2019). The fight over the wall is a budgetary allocation but can also be framed in moral terms. While the gas tax – the issue at stake in the survey of state legislators – is not typically thought of as a moral issue, messages can be framed to highlight moral considerations, including alleviating damage to the environment or economic burdens. The framing of an issue in moral terms may make individuals less willing to compromise on it.

Legislators have two reasons to become more recalcitrant regarding compromise when an issue is framed in moral terms. First, their own positions and moral commitments may restrain them. Just as members of the public are more likely to reject compromises on moral issues, so might elected officials. Second, an understanding that their constituents are reluctant to compromise on moral issues may deter electorally motivated legislators from compromising as well. Our second hypothesis does not seek to separate these two reasons – legislators' own moral concerns or their concerns about how the electorate would respond to moral considerations – but rather focuses on the question of whether moral framing can affect legislators' willingness to compromise. This leads to the second hypothesis.

Moral Framing Hypothesis: Legislators who receive arguments for policy change framed in moral terms will be more likely to reject compromise proposals.

DENYING THE OPPOSITION PARTY CREDIT EXPLANATION

The electoral costs of accepting a half-loaf compromise may be high if voting for a compromise dilutes the credit a legislator's party can claim for solving the policy problem. As a result, legislators may reject proposals to deny the opposition party credit for passage of legislation. Because legislators rely on their party to create a cohesive reputation that serves their reelection interests (Cox and McCubbins 1993, 2005), legislation that receives bipartisan support can make it difficult for one party to claim credit. As a result, even when a policy change is good for a legislator and her constituents, it may not be good for her party (Cox and McCubbins 1993; Koger 2003; Grynaviski 2010). Regardless of issue content, a legislator may avoid voting for legislation sponsored by the opposition party (Lee 2009, 2016).[2] Rejecting policies that the opposing party has advanced can deny the opposition party an opportunity to develop a positive reputation in that area or to claim credit for popular policies. Compromise legislation may be particularly vulnerable to such dynamics because the policy improvement is modest and therefore fails to outweigh the political advantages of maintaining disagreements (Gilmour 1995). This leads to our third hypothesis.

> *Denying Credit Hypothesis*: Legislators will be more likely to reject proposals, including compromise proposals, when the bill sponsors come from the opposing party or are bipartisan than when the sponsors are all from the legislator's party.

THE EXPECTATION OF FUTURE POWER EXPLANATION

Legislators may also reject compromise if they expect to be in a better position to get their preferred outcome in the future (Volden 1998). Compromising now may make it harder for a legislator to get all of what she wants in future sessions for several reasons. First, the compromise proposal might become a status quo point that is more difficult to move than the current status quo (Krehbiel 1998; Brady and Volden 1998; Penn 2009). Second, a change now could make it harder to achieve future changes because of friction due to institutional design (Jones et al. 2003) or transaction costs (North 1990). More broadly, legislators may

---

[2] Legislative leaders also have incentives to prioritize policy content that reflects partisan disagreement, either in an effort to enact favored policies (Harbridge 2015) or to engage in messaging to their base even when they know legislation will fail (Lee 2016; Koger and Lebo 2017). This type of agenda-setting may remove from consideration many potential compromises between members of the two parties.

not want to support a change in the present that could constrain their options in the future; changing policy now and then seeking further changes later may take attention away from other important issues on the agenda (Workman et al. 2009). We do not differentiate between these potential reasons in our analyses but rather test the basic expectation that legislators who expect that more legislators who share their issue positions will be in office in the future will be more likely to reject compromise. We tried to make it clear to legislators that we were discussing legislation in the context of a single-round game, which should minimize the impact of the future power, but we still test a fourth hypothesis.

> *Future Power Hypothesis*: Legislators who expect that more legislators serving in the future will share their preferences will be more likely to reject compromises.

PREDICTING WHO REJECTS COMPROMISE AMONG STATE LEGISLATORS AND CITY OFFICIALS

The same surveys presented in Chapter 2 were used to test the four hypotheses about what might drive rejection of half-loaf offers with a combination of experimental manipulations and self-reported information. We tested the *denying credit* and *moral framing* hypotheses by manipulating parts of the vignette that we provided to the legislators. Nearly all state legislators encounter legislation sponsored by the majority or minority party, or by members from both parties. Similarly, legislators encounter a range of moral and amoral justifications for policy. The manipulation of these two factors, therefore, falls within the types of experiences legislators have had and we can expect them to respond to this information as they would in the context of policymaking. We tested the *voter punishment* and *future power* hypotheses by seeing whether legislators' self-reported beliefs correlated with their response to the compromise proposal. The factors that capture respondents' electoral environment and future perceptions are not easily randomized, and we would have risked losing external validity if we asked respondents to consider a hypothetical situation that they have never experienced themselves. Moreover, removing legislators' lived experiences from their answers would have muddied the very insights we hoped to gain about how legislators' actual experiences and perceptions shape their response to compromise. Thus, we allowed legislators to report their own assessments of the degree to which they would face voter retribution for compromise and the likelihood that more legislators who share their issue positions will be in office in the future.

OPPOSITION TO COMPROMISE AMONG STATE LEGISLATORS

To assess the *voter punishment hypothesis*, we asked the legislators how likely voters would be to punish them if they compromised. Specifically, we asked legislators: "In general, if you were to make compromises on policy, how much retribution would you face from voters in your district?" with the response options: None, Some, A lot.[3] These responses were turned into indicator variables for those who expected high voter retribution and some voter retribution, with the omitted category indicating those who thought they would face no voter retribution.

To test the *moral framing hypothesis,* we randomized whether one of the sponsors in the vignette made an argument using moral language. The moral argument treatment (for either a decrease or increase in the gas tax) included several words that are associated with moral considerations in decision-making along a care/harm dimension (moral, preserve, protect, dangerous, harm, and caring [Graham et al. 2009]). We pre-tested several variations of the moral and amoral argument language with members of the public on Amazon's Mechanical Turk[4] to ensure that the messages differed in the extent of moral framing without affecting argument strength.[5] Based on the results of the pre-tests, we selected the following treatments. For those who wanted to *increase the gas tax* in their state (relative to the status quo), we randomly displayed one of the following arguments:

---

[3] We asked these questions about voter punishment and future power after the vignette to avoid priming or inducing demand effects.

[4] This service allows small payments to workers in the US public for completing tasks. In this case, we used these workers to evaluate the degree to which arguments were strong and focused on moral considerations.

[5] Specifically, we pre-tested several possible treatments using respondents from Amazon's Mechanical Turk to ensure that we presented arguments in the treatments that were (1) perceived as having differing degrees of moral language, (2) perceived as being of similar strength, and (3) the same across the increase and decrease gas tax choices. For our pre-test, we gave each of the 1,639 MTurk respondents one argument from among five possible arguments in favor of a compromise position between their ideal position and the status quo. The five arguments were slightly different versions of the moral or amoral language. We then asked respondents whether "The legislator is trying to make an ethical appeal to listeners" and whether "The legislator makes a strong argument" on a five-point scale from "Strongly Disagree" to "Strongly Agree." The sets of statements used here met all of the three criteria noted above. For both increases and decreases to the gas tax, the moral treatment messages were perceived as making an appeal rooted more in ethical consideration than the amoral messages. On the other hand, the moral and amoral treatment messages used here were perceived as similarly strong. The selected language was the only pairing that met criteria (1) and (2) across both the increase and decrease arguments.

Moral treatment: "Climate change is a dangerous problem with important moral implications. We must act on our obligation to preserve the earth and protect future generations from harm. This proposal is not perfect, but it is a step towards caring for the environment."

Amoral treatment: "Climate change is a problem with important implications. This proposal is not perfect, but it is a step towards improving the environment."

For those who wanted to *decrease the gas tax*, we randomly displayed one of the following arguments:

Moral treatment: "Slow economic growth is a dangerous problem with important moral implications. We must act on our obligation to preserve jobs and protect future generations from harm. This proposal is not perfect, but it is a step towards caring for the economy."

Amoral treatment: "Slow economic growth is a problem with important implications. This proposal is not perfect, but it is a step towards improving the economy."

To evaluate the *denying the opposition credit* hypothesis, we randomized the partisanship of the bill's two sponsors so that legislators saw one of three conditions: two Democrats, two Republicans, or a Republican and a Democrat. Figure 3.1 displays the full vignette. For the analysis, we

---

Suppose that [two Democratic legislators / two Republican legislators / a Republican legislator and a Democratic legislator] in your state proposed a bill that would only affect the state gas tax, and would set the new state gas tax to {X} cents per gallon, a {Y} cent {increase/decrease}.

Recall that the current gas tax in {STATE} is about {SQ GAS TAX} cents per gallon and you stated a preference for {THEIR STATED PREFERENCE} cents per gallon.

In proposing the bill, one of the sponsoring legislators argued:
[MORAL ARGUMENT TEXTS]

Would you vote for this bill if it were introduced in your legislature?
   Yes
   No

FIGURE 3.1. Text of half-loaf compromise vignette.
Note: The text given in square brackets varied randomly across legislators. The text given in curly brackets was taken or calculated from legislators' prior answers or from current policy. This convention is used throughout this book. X is the midpoint between the status quo and the legislator's preferred policy. Y is the distance between the current gas tax and the proposed gas tax and is calculated automatically as | (SQ GAS TAX – STATED PREFERENCES)/2 |.

create indicator variables for opposition sponsors and bipartisan sponsors, with the omitted category indicating same-party sponsors, to evaluate whether a greater potential for opposition party credit decreases the likelihood of compromising.

To assess the *future power hypothesis,* we asked respondents for their perception of how much power legislators who share their view on this issue would have in the future. Given the partisan and demographic patterns across states, some legislators are essentially permanent members of the minority. Others have only served over a couple of years where things are looking better and better for their party or those who otherwise share their views. Rather than risk losing important insights from legislators' actual experiences by randomizing future power or asking them to consider a hypothetical situation, we use legislators' self-reports about their future expectations. Respondents had five options for the amount of future power: a lot more, a little more, the same amount of power, a little less, and a lot less. For the analysis, we use a continuous variable on a five-point scale.[6]

Per the pre-analysis plan, the regression predicting legislators' support for the half-loaf compromise also controls for the legislators' gender, their partisanship, whether they were in the majority in their chamber, and magnitude of the policy change. The distance of the proposal from the status quo (which equals the absolute value of the legislator's induced preference minus the status quo gas tax) holds constant the magnitude of the policy change being offered to the legislators. Figure 3.2 presents the coefficients, which can be interpreted as the change in likelihood that a legislator supports the compromise, and 90% confidence intervals from the OLS regression model to test the hypotheses. These confidence intervals correspond to one-sided tests at the 0.05 level, which match the directional hypotheses we examine in this chapter and which we laid out in the pre-analysis plan. We use a linear probability model to ease the interpretation of the results, but the findings using a probit model are similar.

The results show that legislators who fear *voter punishment* are more likely to reject half-loaf compromises. Legislators who believe that their voters are very likely "to punish legislators engaging in policy compromise" are 21 percentage points less likely to vote yes on the compromise than those who do not think they will face retribution ($p = 0.045$, one-sided). This relationship captures legislators' perceptions of punishment

---

[6] The results are similar if this variable is treated as a factor variable instead.

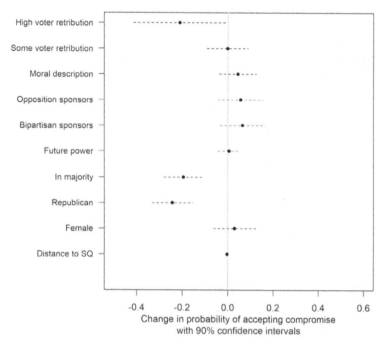

State Legislators

FIGURE 3.2. Predictors of compromise among state legislators.
Note: Coefficients from OLS regression that also includes a constant. $N = 257$, R-Squared = 0.17.

above and beyond the ways that voter preferences shape their induced policy preferences in the first place.

The results regarding fear of voter retribution, however, could be due to mismatches between voters' preferences and the legislator's preferences on the compromise policy if legislators are not fully incorporating the preferences of voters into their reported preferred gas tax. As discussed in Chapter 2, we separately asked them for the preferences of voters in their district in the question eliciting their preferred gas tax level (for more details, see Anderson et al. 2016). In robustness checks not reported here, we control for whether the legislator's ideal policy is on the other side of the status quo from what she reported to be her voters' ideal policy. Even controlling for this mismatch, legislators who report more fear of voter retribution reject compromise more often; it is not just those legislators who are on the opposite side of the status quo from their voters who refuse to compromise. More generally, legislators who report that their voters' preferred policy is more distant from the compromise proposal are not more likely to reject it. These combined patterns indicate that fear of retribution for compromising captures something beyond constituents' policy preferences and potential mismatches between a legislator and her constituents.

The regression results provide no evidence for the other three hypotheses. The empirical evidence shows that framing arguments for the policy in moral terms does not significantly predict voting against the half-loaf compromise. While legislators may still be less likely to compromise on issues that are *inherently* moral in nature, it suggests that *framing* arguments to make moral considerations salient does not affect legislators' willingness to compromise.

Expectations about future positioning in the legislature also do not predict legislators' likelihood of compromising. Those who think legislators who share their policy views would gain power in the future are just as likely to reject the half-loaf compromise as those who think legislators who share their view would lose power in the future.

Finally, legislators do not respond to proposals sponsored by opposition legislators or bipartisan legislators any differently than those sponsored by members of their own party. Although legislators recognize that the party of the sponsors affects the credit each party can claim, legislators do not appear to be concerned about the opposition party getting credit for passing a bill. After the question on how they would vote on the proposal, we asked legislators how much credit their party would get if the bill passed on a scale ranging from 0 to 100%. This measure of credit is used to test if the mechanism we posit, the denial of credit for legislative success, at work. Consistent with the assumption that the sponsoring party affects credit, the legislators think that their party will get less credit if the opposition sponsors the bill (see Table 3.1). When legislators from the opposing party sponsor the bill, legislators, on average, believe that their party will get approximately 11 percentage points less credit for passing the bill than if members of their own party sponsor it. While legislators recognize that sponsorship affects the reputation of the party as a whole, this collective credit for one's own party or the opposing party does not affect whether the legislator supports or rejects the half-loaf compromise. Simply put, legislators do not reject half-loaf compromises because the compromise would assign credit to the opposing party.

The control variables show a mix of insignificant and significant effects. The magnitude of the change that the legislator wanted does not affect willingness to compromise; legislators who want a much higher or

TABLE 3.1. *Effect of sponsorship on credit*

Dependent Variable = Credit for Own Party	(1)
Opposition sponsors	−10.9*
	(4.5)
Bipartisan sponsors	−2.8
	(4.5)
Intercept	60.7*
	(3.4)
N	227
R-Squared	0.029

Note: The dependent variable ranges from 0 to 100 and measures anticipated share of credit to respondent's party. Model estimated using OLS regression. Standard errors in parentheses.

* $p < 0.05$ (one-sided).

much lower gas tax than the one already in place are no more likely to refuse the compromise than those who seek a smaller change. Similarly, the legislator's gender has no impact on whether he or she supports or rejects the half-loaf compromise.

Two of the control variables were significant predictors of legislator support for compromise: partisanship and majority status. Regarding the finding that Republicans are more likely to reject compromise, it is tempting to ascribe this pattern to legislators' efforts to appease Republican voters, as surveys suggest they are more likely to oppose compromise than Democratic voters (Pew 2012). However, the voter retribution measure already captures perceptions of opposition to compromise within each district (and thus any resulting party differences).

A second possibility is that the Republican effect comes from other aspects of the party organization and identity, which differ across the two parties (Grossmann and Hopkins 2015). At both the elite and mass levels, the Republican Party values ideological purity while the Democratic Party is, as Grossmann and Hopkins (2015, 121) explain, essentially "a coalition of social groups seeking concrete government action." Building on this logic, Republicans may be less likely to compromise because of the coalition's emphasis on ideological purity. Similarly, the Democratic focus on interest group politics might make Democratic legislators more open to making trade-offs between groups to get outcomes that make incremental improvements.

That legislators in the majority party reject half-loaf offers more often is also surprising. These majority party legislators are not rejecting compromise because majority status conveys something about who will hold power in the future; the regression includes controls for their future expectations of power. Instead, perhaps legislators in the majority have different experiences achieving their most preferred policies versus being forced to accept compromise proposals. Because majority party legislators have more success advancing their legislative initiatives (Volden and Wiseman 2014), they may have to compromise less and so may be less willing to do so. When we probed state legislators in open-ended questions at the NCSL Summit, one member of the minority said that "legislators in the minority party are keen to compromise when the majority asks because it makes them feel relevant" (2017 NCSL Attendee 180). Selection might also lead to this result. The people who choose to run for a party that will be in the minority may be people who are willing to compromise (because otherwise they do not expect to get much done), while the majority party might entice potential candidates who expect to get their way while in office and who do not expect to have to compromise (Thomsen 2017).

The conclusions regarding the four hypotheses do not change when controlling for four additional factors that go beyond the controls indicated in our pre-analysis plan: the legislator's vote share in the previous election, whether the state was experiencing divided government, the size of the majority party in the legislator's chamber, and a dummy variable for whether the legislator wanted a gas tax increase. Again, the only significant predictor is whether the legislator believes that voters punish legislators who compromise, and the coefficient is even larger in magnitude (a coefficient of -0.27, with $p = 0.018$, one-sided).

In sum, the results of the survey of state legislators suggest that fear of voter retribution is a key factor that explains why some legislators reject half-loaf offers. As described below, a follow-up study with city officials confirms this result and shows that it also applies in other electoral and institutional environments.

OPPOSITION TO COMPROMISE AMONG CITY OFFICIALS

Our second study adapts the survey of state legislators to the city context. As described in Chapter 2, we asked 1,440 city officials to pick one area of the budget they thought should get a greater share of the budget than it does now, one area that should receive a smaller share of the budget, and one area that should be kept the same. We then assigned them to a bargaining scenario over one of these areas. If the officials were assigned to an issue where they wanted to change spending, they were told that about half of the city officials wanted to keep spending at the previous year's level. If the officials were assigned to an issue where they wanted to keep spending the same, they were told that about half the officials wanted to change spending.

As with the state legislators, the study of city officials was designed to test whether officials reject compromise and whether perceived *voter retribution* for compromise and expectations of *future power* predict officials' willingness to compromise. This study did not vary the partisanship of the sponsor or the degree of moral considerations in arguments for the legislation. Neither variable was significant in the survey of state legislators, and it would have been difficult to randomize partisan sponsorship in the context of city officials and budgetary spending. Many city positions are explicitly non-partisan, making it difficult to theorize about how the partisanship of sponsors would affect decisions and unrealistic to implement for officials in non-partisan bodies.

We used the same question for legislators and for city officials to test the impact of voter retribution: "In general, if you were to make compromises on policy, how much retribution would you face from voters in your district?" with the response options: None, Some, A lot. To test the effect of an official's expectations about future power, we asked respondents for their perception of how much power city officials who share their view on this issue would have in the city in the future: "Elections change the composition of voting bodies. Thinking about this issue and your city, which of the following best describes what you expect in the future? Officials who share my views on the level of spending on {ASSIGNED ISSUE} will…" They were given five options ranging from "gain a lot more power in the city" to "lose a lot of power in the city," which we treat as a continuous variable in the analysis.

We also include variables for the official's self-reported partisanship (those who self-identified as Democrats are the omitted/baseline category in the regression) and whether the city official is usually in the majority voting bloc. Many city officials work in non-partisan groups and thus do not have a formal majority or minority party. Therefore, we proxied being in the majority voting bloc by asking "When you vote on formal motions in your capacity as a city leader, how often are you on the winning side?"

City Officials

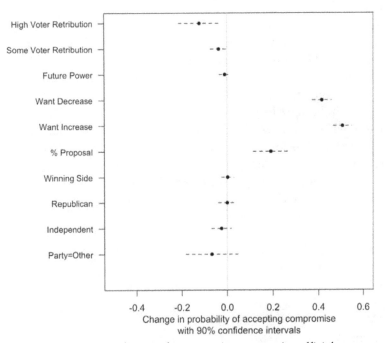

FIGURE 3.3. Predictors of compromise among city officials.
Note: Coefficients from OLS regression that also includes a constant. $N = 1440$, R-Squared = 0.26.

Figure 3.3 presents the coefficients and 90% confidence intervals from an OLS regression model predicting support for the half-loaf compromise. Like state legislators, city officials who report fear of voter retribution for compromising are more likely to reject compromise. City officials who expect to face high voter punishment for compromising are 12 percentage points less likely to vote for the half-loaf compromise than those who do not expect to be punished for compromise ($p = 0.015$, one-sided), and those who think they will face some voter punishment are 4 percentage points less likely to compromise ($p = 0.049$, one-sided). This replicates the results from the *voter punishment hypothesis* in the state legislator analysis. As with state legislators, expectations of *future power* do not have a significant impact on-city officials' willingness to support the proposal.

As noted in Chapter 2, city officials recognize the different incentives to compromise that exist when they prefer the status quo versus want to change policy. Officials who want to change the status quo are 40–50 percentage points more likely to accept the compromise than those who

wanted to keep the status quo. This pattern suggests that officials understand the basic logic of the compromise in the survey experiment and
also highlights the role that defenders of the status quo play in limiting
support for compromises (Baumgartner et al. 2009).

The favorability of the compromise also mattered. City officials who
received a compromise that represented 90% of what they had sought
are 15 percentage points more likely to accept the compromise than officials who were offered 10 percentage points of what they wanted. This
indicates that city officials grasp the details of the compromise offered to
them and respond more favorably when it is closer to their ideal policy.

In contrast to state legislators, partisan differences do not arise in
the city official population. City officials often do not share the same
strength of alignment with the party as their state or national colleagues.
These officials also often deal with less partisan issues than state or
national legislators. These differences may explain why partisanship
does not affect acceptance of compromise among city officials. Similarly,
those on the winning side more often are not more or less likely to vote
for compromise.

The results of both studies highlight the importance of perceived voter
retribution in exacerbating gridlock by driving officials to reject compromises. In two different institutional environments, officials' fear of
voter punishment leads them to reject compromises. Elected officials at
multiple levels of government worry about voter retribution for compromising on public policy, and greater fear drives these officials to reject
compromises that benefit them on policy grounds.

DISCUSSION

This chapter used surveys of state legislators and city officials to test
the reasons that legislators reject compromises even when the proposal
moves policy toward their most preferred outcome. These officials
reject half-loaf offers up to a quarter of the time and do so, in part,
because of how they view their constituents. Among both state legislators and city officials, those who expect to be punished for compromise are more likely to vote against half-loaf compromise proposals.
These findings suggest that the tension between legislators' policy and
electoral interests is important to resolving the puzzle of why so many
legislators reject compromises. While theories of legislative organization and behavior often emphasize legislators' multiple goals, how
legislators resolve this tension is not always addressed (see Koger and

Lebo 2017 for a good overview of this challenge). In the case of under-standing legislators' rejection of compromise, this tension is critical. Legislators reject compromise when they have strong electoral incentives to oppose it, even though that decision leaves them worse off on policy grounds.

The findings of this chapter leave open many questions, particularly about what legislators mean when they say that their voters are likely to punish compromise. Are they thinking of the primary electorate for their party (Boatright 2013; Sherman 2014)? Are they thinking of donors and other elite actors who may shape their electoral prospects (Bonica 2013; La Raja and Schaffner 2015)? Or, do they believe punishment is widespread among the general electorate? Political science scholarship provides abundant data about how the electorate views elected officials – through large-scale data collection in the American National Election Study and the Cooperative Congressional Election Survey, as well as polling from Gallup, Pew, and others. Yet, we know relatively little about how legislators view the public (for exceptions, see Kull and Destler 1999; Broockman and Skovron 2018). Chapter 4 examines these questions by focusing on legislator perceptions of voters and on legislators' roll call votes.

4

Primary Voters as the Source of Punishment

In my state primary voters are probably the biggest deterrent to legislative compromise.

2017 NCSL Attendee 50

For legislators concerned with reelection, support for a legislative compromise needs to be good politics, not just good policy. Legislators should prefer the types of proposals we offered them over the status quo, as they move policy toward what they want. But moving policy only partway may not be good politics. To the extent that voters (or a key subset of voters) are perceived to oppose compromise itself, legislators who are electorally attuned to the preferences of these voters may also oppose compromise policies, even when the proposals move policy toward their preferred outcome. In the studies discussed in Chapter 3, 72% of state legislators and 68% of elected city officials thought they would receive some or a lot of retribution if they compromised. As one attendee at NCSL put it, a reason to reject a half-loaf compromise is "The realization that [in accepting compromises] people will go against their base, lose funding support, and ultimately lose an election" (2017 NCSL Attendees 231).

In Chapter 3, we showed that elected officials who think that their voters will punish compromise are more likely to reject half-loaf compromises. This suggests that legislators may feel constrained by the electorate in ways that extend beyond taking voters into account when they report their induced preferences on a policy issue (Miller and Stokes 1963). But what do legislators mean when they say that voters are likely to punish compromise? Are they thinking of all voters, or a subset of voters? There are many ways that voters can punish elected officials when they disapprove of their support for compromise – voting for primary or general election opponents, not voting, funding negative campaigns against the legislator, and withholding donations. Do they fear electoral punishment in a general election, or is this fear concentrated in the primary election, where another member from their own party may challenge their commitment to party principles (Brady et al. 2007; Boatright 2013)? Are legislators who face primary voters who are vocal in their opposition to compromise more likely to reject compromise proposals? Or is it a concern about even more narrow groups – donors and organized interests (Bawn et al. 2012; La Raja and Schaffner 2015)? Our survey question in Chapter 3 did not specify which group of voters legislators fear, leaving open many possibilities. In this chapter, we focus on three groups that can affect legislators' reelection efforts: general election voters, primary election voters, and campaign donors.

One cautionary tale that many legislators today may be cognizant of points toward primary voters: Eric Cantor's primary election defeat at the hands of a Tea Party challenger in 2014. At the time, Cantor, a Republican from Virginia, was in his 14th year in Congress and was serving as the House Majority Leader. He had won seven successive general elections with between 58 and 75% of the votes. In his 2014 primary election, Cantor outspent his opponent, Dave Brat, by a large margin and Cantor's internal polling showed him leading by more than 30%. But he lost by nearly 10%.

Observers at the time suggested several reasons for Cantor's loss. Some thought Cantor was losing touch with his district and spending too much time in Washington. Others thought that Cantor's leadership position and subsequent policy positions in favor of compromise had been a significant factor. After moving into a leadership position in the House, Cantor had taken more moderate positions that reflected a willingness to work across the aisle. For example, he worked with Democrats to try to pass a compromise immigration overhaul bill. His opponent, Dave Brat, seized on this fact and effectively branded Cantor as a sellout. Brat characterized Cantor's negotiations with Democrats on the bill as evidence that he was in "cahoots" with Democrats (Memoli 2014).

While there are likely multiple factors behind Cantor's loss, several Republicans saw his defeat as a lesson that they should avoid compromise. Congressman Lee Terry, a Republican from Nebraska, stated that Cantor's loss conveyed the message to fellow Republicans that "negotiations or compromises can get you beat" (Sanchez 2014). Whatever combination of factors led to Cantor's stunning loss, it is significant that fellow legislators saw the punishment of compromise as a key factor when they tried to read the proverbial tea leaves following his defeat. It was a strong signal to many legislators that compromising can hurt you electorally.

In this chapter, we use additional survey evidence to assess whether legislators attribute the punishment they would face for compromise to general election voters, primary election voters, or campaign donors. To assess whether the fear of voter punishment that legislators report shapes voting behavior, we consider roll call votes in the US Congress, studying whether legislators whose voters are more attached to the Tea Party, a group that explicitly rejected compromise and targeted legislators in primary elections, are more likely to oppose compromise legislation in Congress. Our findings point to primary elections as the source of punishment for compromising; a pattern that is evident in legislators' perceptions and in their observed behavior.

GENERAL ELECTION VOTERS

The general election is the main event that incumbents need to win. Politicians who are single-minded seekers of reelection (Mayhew 1974) care about voters in the general election because they need a plurality of their votes to win office. Elected officials must cater to the preferences of their general election voters or risk losing in the next election (Canes-Wrone et al. 2002). As one NCSL attendee said, a legislator's decision "[a]lways comes back to constituents" (2017 NCSL Attendee 118). Thus, if politicians fear that compromise will hinder their chances in the general election – whether by shifting votes to the opposing candidate or discouraging voters from turning out – this would likely drive their avoidance of compromise. But despite the importance of the general electorate to reelection, there are three reasons to believe this group of voters is not who legislators have in mind when they express a concern about being punished for compromising.

First, many incumbents do not face a serious challenger in the general election. At both the national and state level, the vast majority of races are safe for one political party (Abramowitz 2010) and voters are increasingly well sorted into political parties and vote accordingly (Levendusky 2009). In this electoral environment, few incumbents worry about strong general election challenges from the opposing party and voters simply follow party cues in the general election, giving the dominant party candidate the victory. In the 2016 election cycle, for example, 42% of state legislative races did not have candidates from both of the major political parties (Ballotpedia 2016b). Moreover, many of the challengers who run against incumbents are weak candidates (Jacobson and Kernell 1983). Many legislators have little to fear in the general election.

Second, and more importantly, the pivotal centrist voters in general election contests likely favor compromise. These swing voters are unlikely to systematically punish legislators for compromising. General election voters are made up of partisans from the incumbent's party, independents, and partisans from the challenger's party. While strong partisans may not want legislative compromise from their own party, independents and weak partisans are much more supportive of compromise and bipartisanship (Harbridge and Malhotra 2011; Wolak 2013; Harbridge et al. 2014). Voters from the opposing party are all the more likely to value bipartisanship and compromise (Paris 2017), although they are unlikely to vote for the legislator in any case. Thus, legislators are unlikely to lose the general election because voters who are pivotal in the general election – likely independents or weak partisans – punish them for compromising.

The third reason legislators are unlikely to fear punishment for compromise from general election voters is that surveys show such voters are unlikely to pay sufficient attention to politics to punish legislators for compromising. For instance, in the 2016 American National Election Study (Hutchings et al. 2017), primary voters consumed significantly more media about national politics than general election voters who did not vote in the primary.[1] General election voters are generally less knowledgeable about politics than more politically attentive groups like donors and primary voters (Delli Carpini and Keeter 1996). As a result, general election voters are less likely to know about the votes of the incumbent, especially enough about specific roll call votes to punish the incumbent for voting for a particular compromise proposal. Absent this information about particular votes and legislators' support of compromise, general election voters are likely to follow party cues (Bartels 2000).

---

[1] On a 0–4 scale, mean media consumption was 2.8 among primary voters versus 2.4 among general election only voters ($p < 0.001$, two-sided).

PRIMARY ELECTION VOTERS

Incumbents have more reasons to worry about the response to compromise from voters in their primary election than they do from voters in the general election because primary voters are more averse to compromise, more likely to know and use legislator's voting records in their voting decisions, and because primary elections may loom large in the calculus of winning office. Legislators appear to recognize this. In answering a question about whether they could name a time when someone lost a seat because of legislative compromise, one attendee at the 2017 NCSL said that it would be more likely to happen "in a contested primary, not a general election" (2017 NCSL Attendee 35).

Primary voters' opposition to compromise goes beyond pure ideological concerns.[2] Unlike the pivotal centrist voters in the general election, many of the strong partisans who vote in primaries do not support bipartisanship or, presumably, the compromises it entails (Harbridge and Malhotra 2011; Harbridge et al. 2014). While partisan strength or ideological extremity may not always imply opposition to compromise, some research suggests there is often lower support for compromise among the most ideologically extreme (Pew 2014a). Some primary voters may even view their side as absolutely correct. As *Washington Post* columnist Robert J. Samuelson summarizes, "the curse of U.S. politics is that it's become less about interests and more about ideologies – and ideologies breed moral absolutes, rigid agendas and strong emotions" (Samuelson 2013). If legislators perceive primary voters as opposed to compromise, they may be responsive to these preferences.

Because candidates generally share a party affiliation with their primary voters, their legislative record may be more central in primary elections where voters cannot rely on party labels as a cue. In addition to holding

---

[2] Primary voters take positions that are more extreme than those taken by voters in the general election and are even more extreme than the supporters voting for the party in the general election (Hill 2015). Thus, pleasing primary voters would tend to pull legislators toward the extremes (Burden 2001). However, not all scholars find that primary voters are sophisticated enough to identify more or less extreme candidates in primary elections (Ahler et al. 2016) or that primaries drive polarization (Hirano et al. 2010; Boatright 2013, 2014). Our focus in this chapter is on legislators' beliefs about various groups of voters, which are important because these beliefs lead to action. We return to the question of whether primary voters are more likely to punish compromise in Chapter 5.

strong views, primary voters are more likely pay attention to their legislator's voting record, especially on issues about which they care deeply, giving them the knowledge necessary to punish the legislator for compromising. This can make votes for compromise more consequential in contested primaries.

Primary voters also loom large in the electoral calculus. Many state and federal districts are safe for one party, moving competition from the general election to the primary election stage (Carson et al. 2011a, 2012) and making the primary election the key electoral context. Especially as districts have become safer for one party due to redistricting and geographic sorting (Carson et al. 2007), "sometimes, the constituency that matters is the 'primary constituency'" (Squire and Moncrief 2015, 162). In the most extreme cases of one-party control, "[t]he primary is the election" (Key 1949, 407). In this context, legislators would like to avoid the emergence of a strong primary challenger. Support for compromise proposals might frustrate primary voters and open the door for a successful challenger. Challengers can make a compromise vote into a campaign issue and they can claim that they would have worked to get the whole loaf; painting the incumbent as a sellout, unprincipled, or in cahoots with the opposing party. The ability of a primary challenger to run against a legislator's support for compromises also suggests that even if only a subset of the primary electorate punishes a legislator for compromising, a legislator may worry that this group may help recruit or support a primary challenger, who can then seek to rally a larger set of voters.

The counterargument against the influence of primaries is the simple, observed fact that incumbents rarely lose in primaries. In 2016, only 5 (1.3%) incumbent House members lost their party's nomination (Ballotpedia 2016c). Likewise only 123 (around 2.5%) incumbent state legislators lost their primary election (Ballotpedia 2016a).

Yet it may be legislators' very responsiveness to primary voters that keeps them in office. Incumbents are reelected at high rates, despite the threat they face, exactly because they take the threat seriously and respond accordingly. They keep a pulse on primary voters' preferences and work to keep them happy (Fenno 1978). Incumbents want to avoid strong challenges and may change their behavior to accommodate primary voters' views. For instance, Senator John McCain (R-AZ) changed his position on climate change in 2009 in the face of a far-right primary challenge from J.D. Hayworth (Rosenbluth and Shapiro 2018, 102). Even though incumbents rarely lose, legislators who are mindful of reelection will be cautious and responsive to this subset of the electorate.

Legislators may be particularly concerned if they see others lose in primary elections. After seeing fellow Senator Bob Bennett (R-UT) lose a party convention fight to Tea Party candidate Mike Lee, Senator Orrin Hatch (R-UT) moved to the right and sought to court Tea Party activists (Karol 2015, 76). In another example, one NCSL attendee reported that

> In Idaho, [the] alt-right targeted moderate Republicans for compromising and ran negative campaigns to remove them. Merrill Beyeler in Idaho, a great leader, was seen as too compromising and [the] "tea party" spent a lot of money to un-elect him. Very sad day for our state because of his knowledge of land management. This scenario has occurred numerous times in Idaho. A good case study of "fights" with the party. (2017 NCSL Attendee 175, for more details see Barker 2016)

Such primary losses may have encouraged other legislators to heed the wishes of primary voters and avoid compromising, lest they be the next member targeted. Legislators may respond to these primary election incentives by seeking to align themselves with primary voters (Brady et al. 2007). If they believe these voters, or even an important subset of them, will punish them for compromising, they may be more likely to reject half-loaf offers.

CAMPAIGN DONORS

In addition to worrying about the citizens who vote in primary and general elections, incumbents need money to compete. Raising money allows incumbents to run the campaigns that mobilize their supporters and persuade swing voters. Further, raising funds is one way that incumbents can deter strong challengers from entering the race (Epstein and Zemsky 1995; Olivella et al. 2017). The highest quality challengers tend to be more strategic and so run when conditions are favorable (Jacobson 2014). When incumbents raise more money they signal that they enjoy strong support and will be tough to beat. Thus, raising enough funds can help incumbents deter quality challengers from entering the primary and general election races.

While incumbents have strong incentives to vote in ways that help them raise more funds (Fox and Rothenberg 2011; Jansa and Hoyman 2018), there is mixed evidence on how that pressure should affect politicians' willingness to compromise. Like general election voters, campaign donors are made up of distinct subgroups that may take very different positions regarding compromise. While Bonica (2013) concludes that many interest groups have moderate positions and are focused on gaining access rather than putting pressure on legislators to take extreme positions (see also Hansen 1991; Harden and Kirkland 2016), others find that activists in the public who contribute money are quite ideological themselves and are dramatically more focused on the ideological extremity of candidates than are political parties when donating to candidates (La Raja and Schaffner 2015; Barber 2016). These views may translate into opposition to compromise. For example, donors like the Koch Brothers did not want the "electability-over-principles approach" that they saw establishment Republican strategists like Karl Rove and Ed Gillespie as embodying (Vogel and Smith 2011). They wanted legislators who hold the line on policy at all costs. In their 2017 book decrying polarization in American politics, Senators Trent Lott (R-MS) and Tom Daschle (D-SD) pointed to a similar opposition to compromise from key donors. "There are lots of responsible, conservative senators looking over their shoulders, worried about getting attacked from the Club for Growth or the Senate Conservatives Fund and their deep war chests," they lamented (Lott and Daschle 2017, 42). At least some legislators recognize that compromising could affect their relationship with donors. One NCSL attendee noted that the "[t]hreat of loss of donor support" (2017 NCSL Attendee 200) is a reason to reject half-loaf compromises.

One remaining consideration is how those voters who might punish compromise learn that a legislator compromised. As suggested above, there are significant differences in political media consumption and knowledge between general and primary election voters. Donors are also likely to consume more media and have more knowledge about politics. While interested voters may gather information about legislators' votes on their own, they can also learn about legislators' voting behavior through intermediaries. Interest groups and their activists are one such intermediary (Bawn et al. 2012). Many interest groups score legislators on the degree to which they vote with the positions of the group, with the goal of identifying friends and enemies (Fowler 1982; Snyder 1992). Primary voters and donors who are aligned with a particular interest group are more likely to learn this information and this may open the door for a primary challenger. In the debate over the San Rafael Swell discussed in Chapter 1, the decision by the League of Conservation Voters to score votes on the amendments increased how much scrutiny these votes received. This is an example of a pattern in recent years where groups like the Club for Growth, the League of Conservation Voters, the National Rifle Association, and others negatively "score" congressional votes in support of compromise bills.[3]

---

[3] Many of the calls for "no" votes announced by the Club for Growth in recent years were on bills brought forward by the majority party that were viewed as compromises (www.clubforgrowth.org/category/key-votes/).

For example, soon after the Manchin-Toomey compromise amendment on expanded background checks for firearm purchases failed, Senator Joe Manchin (D-WV) attributed the amendment's doom to the National Rifle Association's announcement that it would score the vote (Baker 2015, 44). Engaged segments of the population may well pay attention to these interest group scores when considering whether to donate to a candidate or to vote for him or her in a primary.

LEGISLATORS FOCUS ON PUNISHMENT BY PRIMARY VOTERS

In August of 2017 we surveyed legislators in person to learn how much their perceptions of these three key constituencies (general election voters, primary election voters, and campaign donors) drive their fear about retribution for compromising. At the 2017 National Conference of State Legislatures (NCSL) in Boston we rented a booth in the exhibition hall under the banner of our universities (Washington University in St. Louis, Northwestern University, and the University of California). During the 18 hours over three days that the exhibit hall was open, two to three members of our research team actively recruited attendees in the hall to stop and take a survey in exchange for a T-shirt. After giving informed consent and agreeing to participate in the research study, state legislators and staffers completed the survey on a tablet and were asked to answer several open-ended questions with pen and paper.

We recruited 366 individuals at NCSL to complete the survey. Of these 215 were state legislators, and the rest were staff members.[4] A disproportionate number of participants came from Hawaii and from the conference's home state of Massachusetts (with each state comprising about 8% of the sample). Still, there was good coverage of most of the United States. For the analysis in this chapter, we limit the sample to the state legislators. Table 4.1 gives the number of respondents in the sample from each state (with the number of legislators given in parentheses).

The survey itself consisted of two parts: several questions with set answers that were administered on tablet computers and then an optional, paper-and-pen portion with several open-ended questions. Among the 366 legislators and staff who participated in the tablet survey,

---

[4] There is a small discrepancy between the numbers in Table 4.1 and the number of observations in the regression analysis because a few people who started the survey did not answer all the questions. Over 95% of the attendees who started the survey completed it, suggesting that the drop off is unlikely to bias the results.

TABLE 4.1. *Number of NCSL 2017 participants by state*

Alabama	3 (2)	Kentucky	15 (8)	North Dakota	2 (0)
Alaska	7 (2)	Louisiana	14 (10)	Ohio	8 (3)
Arizona	6 (3)	Maine	4 (4)	Oklahoma	4 (2)
Arkansas	14 (10)	Maryland	6 (6)	Oregon	4 (2)
California	9 (3)	Massachusetts	28 (12)	Pennsylvania	6 (4)
Colorado	3 (1)	Michigan	6 (2)	Rhode Island	1 (1)
Connecticut	1 (1)	Minnesota	5 (4)	South Carolina	6 (3)
Delaware	2 (2)	Mississippi	13 (13)	South Dakota	9 (4)
DC	3 (0)	Missouri	12 (6)	Tennessee	11 (5)
Florida	4 (2)	Montana	3 (3)	Texas	6 (0)
Georgia	5 (3)	Nebraska	8 (5)	Utah	13 (8)
Hawaii	25 (15)	Nevada	3 (3)	Vermont	10 (8)
Idaho	4 (3)	New Hampshire	11 (10)	Virginia	10 (8)
Illinois	2 (1)	New Jersey	1 (0)	Washington	4 (3)
Indiana	6 (4)	New Mexico	5 (2)	West Virginia	1 (1)
Iowa	0	New York	1 (0)	Wisconsin	9 (5)
Kansas	0	North Carolina	9 (3)	Wyoming	3 (3)

Note: The number in parentheses is the number of surveyed state legislators from the state, while the number not in parentheses includes both legislators and staff. Legislators from 44 states (plus 2 legislators from Puerto Rico, 1 from the Virgin Islands, and 1 from Guam) are included in the analysis.

261 individuals also completed the open-ended portion that followed, in which they were told:

In a recent study, we tested what factors predict when state legislators would reject a compromise bill that moves policy in the direction they prefer, but not all the way to their most preferred outcome. Our main finding was that the threat of punishment from voters was the biggest predictor of rejecting a beneficial, legislative compromise.

They were asked to check yes or no as to whether this fit their understanding of what some legislators experience. The vast majority checked yes. Second, they were asked to name a time when someone lost their seat because they voted for a legislative compromise. Third, they were asked "Thinking back on your legislative experience, are there any other factors that cause legislators to reject beneficial legislative compromises?" Many of the quotes in chapters throughout the book were answers to these two questions. Fourth, they were asked "Is there anything else legislators can do to avoid being punished by voters when they

TABLE 4.2. *Legislators fear retribution for compromise from primary voters most*

	Not at All Likely (%)	Only Slightly Likely (%)	Somewhat Likely (%)	Very Likely (%)
Voters in your party's primary election	9.5	32	43	15
Campaign donors to your party	16	44	29	11
General election voters who don't donate money or vote in a primary	33	40	20	6.2

support compromise bills?" Their answers to this question are discussed in Chapter 7. Finally, they were asked if there is "anything else we should know about the topic of legislative compromise." Some quotes we use in this book also come from this question.

In the tablet portion of the survey, respondents answered the same question about voter retribution for compromise that was included in the experiments in Chapter 3: "In general, if you were to make compromises on policy, how much retribution would you face from voters?" (Answer options: None, Some, A Lot). As in the 2014 survey of legislators, 72% think that they would face some or a lot of retribution. We then asked them whether different groups of voters were "Not at all likely," "Only slightly likely," "Somewhat likely," or "Very likely" to punish compromise, saying "There are many different groups of voters. How likely is each of the following groups to punish a legislator for voting in favor of a compromise bill?" We asked about "Voters in your party's primary election," "Campaign donors to your party," and "General election voters who don't donate money or vote in a primary."[5]

Table 4.2 shows the distribution of responses about how likely legislators think these three groups would be to punish them. The results

---

[5] One issue with recruiting legislators at NCSL is that they may not be representative of all legislators. Legislators who want to meet donors with an eye toward the next election have extra incentive to come because donors sponsor many of the events at NCSL. This may mean that our sample of legislators has a larger percentage of legislators who care about donors than in the population of state legislators as a whole. If this is true of our sample, this feature would likely bias our study toward finding that state legislators are concerned about donors when considering compromises. Instead, we find that even these legislators attending NCSL are most concerned about retribution from primary voters.

show that legislators believe that primary voters were most likely to punish, with 58% stating that they think primary voters would be either somewhat or very likely to punish. They believed that general election voters were the least likely to punish compromise, with only about 26% stating that they think general election voters would be either somewhat or very likely to punish. The donors were in between the other two groups. Further, there is a significant difference between the mean level of perceived punishment from voters in the primary election and voters in the general election, and between voters in the primary election and donors.[6]

To further explore the impact that these groups have on fear of retribution, we use the responses from this question as independent variables in a regression model predicting how much retribution legislators expect to face for compromise (the key predictor of legislators' refusal to compromise in Chapter 3). The variables are on a scale from 0 to 1 to facilitate interpretation of the results.[7]

Table 4.3 presents the results of the OLS regression for the legislators at the 2017 NCSL meeting. The results show that the strongest predictor of legislators' fear of retribution for compromise – and the only one that reaches conventional levels of statistical significance – is fear of punishment by primary voters. By contrast, a belief that general election voters or donors are likely to punish compromise does not predict overall fear of retribution for compromise. When politicians say that they fear punishment for compromising, it appears they fear punishment from primary voters.[8]

[6] The difference in means was calculated by first recoding the fear of retribution to a scale from 0 to 1 with the higher values indicating a greater likelihood of punishment (i.e., "Not at all likely" = 0, "Only slightly likely" = 0.33, "Somewhat likely" = 0.66, and "Very likely" = 1). Among all legislators, the difference in means between primary voters and general election voters is 0.22 ($p < 0.001$, two-sided), and the difference in means between primary voters and donors is 0.10 ($p < 0.001$, two-sided). Both Republicans and Democrats thought that primary voters were more likely to punish a politician for compromise than general election voters. The difference in means is 0.19 for Democrats and 0.27 for Republicans (both $p < 0.001$, two-sided).

[7] The dependent variable equals 0 if they responded "None," 0.5 if they responded "Somewhat," and 1 if they responded "A lot." The independent variables are coded as 0 if they responded "Not likely at all," 0.33 if they responded "Somewhat likely," 0.66 if they responded "Only slightly likely," and 1 if they responded "Very likely."

[8] These results are substantially the same if an ordered logit model is used instead of ordinary least squares. Punishment by primary election voters remains the only significant predictor of fear of voter retribution.

TABLE 4.3. *Punishment by primary voters drives the fear of voter retribution*

Dependent Variable = Fear of Retribution Scale	(1)
Punishment by General Election Voters	0.072
	(0.064)
Punishment by Primary Election Voters	0.14*
	(0.071)
Punishment by Donors	0.069
	(0.072)
Intercept	0.25*
	(0.038)
N	204
R-Squared	0.073

Note: The dependent variable is the level of retribution that the legislator fears when voting for compromise. The dependent variable and the independent variables are recoded to scales ranging from 0 to 1. Model estimated using OLS regression. Standard errors in parentheses.
* $p < 0.05$ (two-sided).

A wave of recent primary challengers on the right from the Tea Party could yield a partisan difference in legislators' perceptions. In the survey, legislators also reported their perceptions that primary voters in the *other* party punish compromise. Democratic legislators do not differentiate between the likelihood of punishment from primary voters in their party and in the Republican Party. The average for primary voters in their own party was 0.52, and the average punishment for primary voters in the other party was 0.55, an insignificant difference ($p = 0.39$, two-sided). By contrast, Republican legislators were significantly more likely to think that primary voters in their party punished legislators for compromising than primary voters in the other party (mean of 0.60 for their own party, mean of 0.42 for the other party, difference of 0.18, $p < 0.001$, two-sided). While legislators from both parties believe that *their* primary voters are more likely to punish compromise than general election voters, Republican legislators seem to believe that they face a primary electorate that is even more averse to compromise than Democrats' primary electorate. NCSL attendees explicitly reported this asymmetry in their open-ended comments as well, with one saying "Yes, fear of being punished in the primary (especially on the Republican side)" is a factor that causes rejection of half-loaf compromises (2017 NCSL Attendee 18). Another said,

Republicans in the early 2000s voted for a tax compromise bill & in the next cycle several were taken out in the primary. Similarly, in the 2015 session at least two Republicans who voted yes on a modest tax (commerce) for education were taken out by more conservative Republicans in primary 2016. Can't think of any Democratic examples. (2017 NCSL Attendee 92)[9]

LEGISLATORS BELIEVE THAT PRIMARY VOTERS OPPOSE LEGISLATIVE COMPROMISE

At the NCSL each respondent also assessed whether primary and general election voters would want a hypothetical member of Congress to support or oppose a proposed compromise. In a vignette, we described a negotiation occurring in Congress. Republicans were presented a vignette about a Republican member of Congress and Democrats were presented a vignette about a Democratic member of Congress. We asked everyone about a member of their own party to evaluate the expectations they had about the subset of voters they know best and who are relevant in primary elections: co-partisans in the public. We also altered the position advocated by the member of Congress in the vignette to correspond to the position on the issue typically taken by those in the respondent's party. The full text of the vignette is given in Figure 4.1. The vignette was *not* a survey experiment; we did not randomly vary any part of the vignette.

In designing the vignette, we purposely created a situation for understanding the dynamics of compromise when it is most consequential and difficult. To make the action of the member of Congress consequential, the vignette indicated that the legislator was pivotal. If the member of Congress voted for the bill, it would pass; if the member of Congress voted against it, the proposal would fail. To represent a situation where voting for compromise is difficult, the vignette indicated that the member of Congress would have to vote against the majority of her party to vote for the compromise proposal. When the legislator's party is already behind the compromise, there is little reason to expect punishment from voters. This may be particularly true if bipartisan agreement equates to unanimous agreement (Druckman et al. 2013; Bolsen et al. 2014; Harbridge et al. 2014). By design the vignette focuses on a situation where the vote is consequential and difficult.

The compromise bill represented half of what the legislator wanted (either in tax increases or spending cuts depending on the legislator's party) without giving up anything in another policy area. This is a

---

[9] This quotation was edited by the authors for clarity. Edits included the names of parties rather than R and D, extending abbreviations of policy areas, and grammatical edits to include definite articles.

We want to learn about how voters respond to the decisions legislators make. Consider a {Republican/Democratic} member of the U.S. Congress. Suppose that Democrats and Republicans in the U.S. Congress have been debating the issue of balancing the budget. After a great deal of disagreement and negotiation by Democrats and Republicans over spending cuts, they voted on a compromise bill that would make about {half of the spending cuts that Republicans/half of the tax increases that Democrats} like this legislator wanted. The vote for the bill is expected to be close, with the majority of the legislator's party opposing the bill. All indications suggest that the legislator's vote will be pivotal. The legislator can either vote in favor of the bill and the bill will pass or can vote against the bill and it will fail. Below are two sets of voters, which decision would make each set most happy?

<u>Voters in the general election</u> would want this legislator to...
    Vote in favor of the bill (and against their party) in order to pass the compromise
    Vote against the bill (and with their party) in order to kill the compromise

<u>Voters who vote in the {Republican/Democratic} primary election</u> would want this legislator to...
    Vote in favor of the bill (and against their party) in order to pass the compromise
    Vote against the bill (and with their party) in order to kill the compromise

FIGURE 4.1. Legislator vignette on voter reactions to compromise proposal. *Note:* Text in curly brackets is programmed to match the party of the respondent and that party's typical preferred means of balancing the budget.

half-loaf compromise where the legislator gets half, but not all, of what she wants – a clear policy win for the legislator.

Most legislators believe that primary voters want the member of Congress to kill compromise bills that are not supported by the majority of their party even if those bills represent a policy position that is closer to the member's preference. Figure 4.2 shows the percentage of legislators who think that each set of voters would want the member to kill the compromise. Legislators' expectations of primary and general election voters' preferences over compromise are wildly different, with a gap of more than 40 percentage points ($p < 0.001$). Only 18% think that general election voters would want the member to kill the compromise. In contrast, 59% of the legislators think that primary election voters would want the member to oppose this compromise. Even when the member of Congress and those who share the member's preferences get half of what they want, most legislators believe that primary voters would want them to reject the half-loaf offer. Together, the results of these two studies at NCSL show that legislators believe primary and general election voters respond differently to compromise and that their resulting concern about voter punishment comes from a fear of primary voters, not general election voters or donors.

In the open-ended questions that followed, legislators at NCSL agreed that the threat of punishment from voters leads them to reject compromise and often mentioned primary voters in particular. When asked what

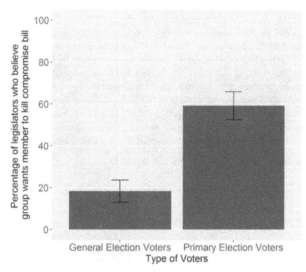

FIGURE 4.2. Legislators' beliefs about voters' preferences for rejecting compromise. *Note:* Bars represent 95% confidence intervals.

factors cause legislators to reject half-loaf compromises, one attendee highlighted "The extreme wings of parties threatening primary challenges" (2017 NCSL Attendee 101). Another emphasized the "Next election threat of a primary" (2017 NCSL Attendee 93). And still others gave specific examples of legislators being punished in the primary for compromise votes, saying "Look at gas tax votes across the country – I think 80% of those who voted for the gas tax have been primaried in the Republican Party" (2017 NCSL Attendee 252) and the "Medicaid Expansion Act compromise cost several legislators their seat due to challenge from right in primary" (2017 NCSL Attendee 5). In sum, legislators believe that primary voters are opposed to compromise and see a connection between voting in support of a compromise and facing a tough primary election.

THE TEA PARTY MOVEMENT AND COMPROMISE

While many legislators fear retribution for compromise from primary voters, over 40% of state legislators reported that primary voters in their district were not at all or only slightly likely to punish compromise. This heterogeneity in expectations of punishment suggests taking a closer look at legislators who have the type of constituency that is likely to punish compromise – those whose primary voters align with groups who have expressed explicit opposition to compromise. An ideal empirical test would compare compromise voting behavior of legislators who face primary voters likely to punish for compromise to legislators who do not face such voters.

The rise of the Tea Party movement offers just such an opportunity, allowing us to assess whether legislators who face primary voters who are more likely to punish compromise are also more hesitant to vote for compromise proposals. In the wake of Obama's inauguration in 2009, the Tea Party movement coalesced around concerns about the size of the federal government and 45 Tea Party-backed candidates won election to Congress in 2010 (Moe 2010). Self-identified Tea Party members in the public share many views of other Republicans (Parker and Barreto 2014), but are slightly more conservative (Abramowitz 2012; Campbell and Putnam 2011; Jacobson 2011). More importantly for our purposes, the Tea Party allows us to study the relationship between fear of voter punishment in primaries and the refusal to support legislative compromises because the Tea Party's demands went beyond having a more conservative ideology and included rhetoric against compromise as a distinguishing trait (Bailey et al. 2012).

From the beginning of the movement, the Tea Party has been a staunch advocate of opposing compromise as a means of pursuing their preferred policies and highlighting their principles. In their interviews with Tea Party groups across the country, Skocpol and Williamson describe Tea Party supporters as people who "would not hear of compromise" (2012, 4) and who sought to "loudly tell Republican officeholders to do what they want or face challenges from the right in the next election" (2012, 101). In a statement typical of the Tea Party viewpoint, Tea Party Patriots co-founder Mark Meckler accused the government of having "compromised our way into disaster" (Hujer and Schmitz 2011). Senator Harry Reid (D-NV) described Tea Party-backed legislators as those who "leave no room for reason or compromise, who don't recognize common ground even when they're standing on it" (Reid 2012). Indeed, as a movement, the Tea Party focused its efforts on primary challenges to Republican incumbents they accused of making compromises with Democrats on important issues. In 2012, Republican Dick Lugar (IN) lost his primary to a Tea Party challenger. As the *Economist* summarized the objections of the Tea Party to Lugar, one of his main sins was his "general inclination to compromise" ("Another moderate shown the door" 2012). Because of this emphasis on refusal to compromise, a larger Tea Party presence should lead Republicans in Congress to be more likely to reject compromise, even holding constant primary voters' ideology.

While most incumbents still win their primaries, the Tea Party has given many reelection-focused politicians pause. High profile losses such as Cantor's and Lugar's may also disproportionately affect the perception of electoral vulnerability. Lugar had represented Indiana for six terms. He noted in his concession speech to Tea Party challenger Richard Mourdock, that

Partisans at both ends of the political spectrum are dominating the political debate in our country. And partisan groups, including outside groups that spent millions against me in this race, are determined to see that this continues. They have worked to make it as difficult as possible for a legislator of either party to hold independent views or engage in constructive compromise. (CNN Political Unit 2012)

The *New York Times* noted that "Mourdock's campaign was fueled by Tea Party groups and national conservative organizations that deemed Mr. Lugar too willing to compromise and poured millions of dollars into the campaign to defeat him" (Davey 2012). Because Republican members of Congress in districts with more Tea Party identifiers have reasons to fear a viable Tea Party primary challenger like Richard Mourdock (Karpowitz et al. 2011), we expect them to be more likely to vote against the types of compromise proposals that Tea Party identifiers dislike.

There is already suggestive evidence that members of Congress who are affiliated with the Tea Party or who have constituents who are active in the Tea Party vote differently from other Republicans, and these patterns are consistent with our expectation that legislators with Tea Party support would reject compromise. Tea Party freshmen (those elected in 2010 with a Tea Party endorsement) opposed President Obama's position on legislation more often than other Republican members of Congress (Bond 2013) and representatives who joined the Tea Party Caucus and had more constituents who registered with Tea Party organizations produced voting records that were distinct from their other Republican counterparts (Ragusa and Gaspar 2016). Similarly, early in the Tea Party era, members of Congress with more Tea Party activists were more likely to vote with the Tea Party position on legislation that was central to the group, such as raising the debt ceiling and the Patriot Act (Bailey et al. 2012). We focus on Republicans in this analysis, but Democrats are not immune to threats from motivated activists (see Associated Press 2018; Siders and Marinucci 2018). The widespread nature of the Tea Party movement simply provides an excellent avenue to examine the consequences of primary voters who oppose compromise. Because the Tea Party focused their efforts only on Republican primaries, we analyze the behavior of the targets of those efforts: incumbent Republicans.

We assess the connection between voter alignment with the Tea Party and legislators' opposition to compromise by turning to the US Congress.

This analysis enables us to test the external validity of the survey findings by studying legislators' observable behavior. The findings earlier in this chapter that legislators fear punishment by primary voters who oppose compromise indicate that members of Congress from districts with larger numbers of Tea Party identifiers should be more likely to vote against compromise proposals. We analyze how the fraction of voters in a district who feel close to the Tea Party affects the willingness of Republican members of Congress to support measures that require compromise during the five years that John Boehner (R-OH) served as Speaker of the House (2011–2015). We focus on this period because these were the years of the Tea Party movement when Republicans were in the majority and thus controlled the agenda. We end the analysis in 2015 because, as part of his deal to become Speaker, Paul Ryan (R-WI) expressed a willingness to alter party rules and the leadership's grip on the legislative process. This deal may have changed the agenda in ways that proactively accommodated legislators who would have opposed compromises had they been brought to a vote (Berman 2015; Binder 2015).

Identifying Compromise Votes

Identifying votes that represent compromise proposals is difficult because we do not know the ideal point of each proposal and the associated status quo. As a result, it is hard to know when a roll call vote represents a half-loaf offer in the form we have discussed thus far – achieving part, but not all, of a legislator's preferred outcome. As a proxy for whether a proposal is a compromise vote more generally, we use the subset of roll call votes that required some minority party votes to pass.

We further limit the sample to key votes from the list produced by *Congressional Quarterly* each year, which captures the most important pieces of legislation on issues ranging from appropriations to tax cuts to education.[10] Over the five years included in the analysis, there were thirty-one such roll call votes. Table 4.4 lists these votes. The dependent variable for the analysis is a binary indicator for whether each Republican legislator voted yes on each roll call vote (1 = yes, 0 = no). For the linear probability model in Table 4.6, we cluster the standard errors by legislator to account for dependence in the error term that comes from using multiple roll call votes from the same set of legislators.

---

[10] https://library.cqpress.com/cqalmanac/toc.php?mode=cqalmanac-appendix&level=2 &values=CQ+Key+Votes+Tables.

TABLE 4.4. *Roll call votes included in the analysis of compromise voting*

Cong	Session	Session Vote #	Bill #	Issue at Stake in Vote	Republican Vote (Yea-Nay)
112	1	46	HR 1	Fiscal 2011 Continuing Appropriations/F-35 Alternative Engine (Rooney Amendment)	110–130
112	1	376	S 990	Patriot Act Extensions	196–31
112	1	491	HR 1249	Patent Overhaul	168–67
112	1	690	S 365	Debt Limit	174–66
112	2	72	HR 3630	Payroll Tax Relief Extension	146–91
112	2	195	HR 4628	Student Loan Interest Rates	202–30
112	2	659	HR 8	Tax Rate Extensions	85–151
113	1	23	HR 152	Disaster Supplemental	49–179
113	1	30	HR 325	Short-Term Debt Limit Increase	199–33
113	1	55	S 47	Violence Against Women Act Reauthorization	87–138
113	1	89	HR 933	Continuing Appropriations	203–27
113	1	125	HR 1765	Air Traffic Controller Furloughs	202–12
113	1	550	HR 2775	Fiscal 2014 Continuing Appropriations and Debt Limit Suspension	87–144
113	1	640	HJRES 59	Fiscal 2014 Budget Agreement	169–62
113	2	21	HR 3547	Fiscal 2014 Omnibus Appropriations	166–64
113	2	31	HR 2642	Farm Programs	162–63
113	2	61	S 540	Debt Limit Extension	28–199

113	2	258	HR 4660	Fiscal 2015 Commerce-Justice-Science Appropriations/Medical Marijuana (Rohrabacher Amendment)	49–172
113	2	322	HR 4870	Defense Appropriations/A-10 Aircraft (Miller Amendment)	155–73
113	2	327	HR 4870	Defense Appropriations/Surveillance (Massie Amendment)	135–94
113	2	452	HCONRES 105	U.S. Military Forces in Iraq	180–37
113	2	507	HJRES 124	Fiscal 2015 Continuing Resolution/Training and Arming Syrian Rebel (McKeon Amendment)	159–71
113	2	563	HR 83	Fiscal 2015 Omnibus Appropriations	162–67
114	1	109	HR 240	Immigration Deportations	75–167
114	1	224	HR 2048	Patriot Act Revision	196–47
114	1	374	HR 2146	Trade Promotion Authority	190–50
114	1	569	HR 597	Export-Import Bank	62–177
114	1	579	HR 1314	Budget Deal	79–167
114	1	665	S 1177	Elementary and Secondary Education	178–64
114	1	673	HR 22	Surface Transportation	178–65
114	1	705	HR 2029	Fiscal 2016 Omnibus Appropriations	150–95

Deeper investigation into the bills illustrates that many of the nay votes represent a rejection of a half-loaf compromise. For example, one of the bills included in the analysis was the 2014 Farm Bill, H.R. 2642. *CQ Almanac* reporting on initial passage of the House version of the bill stated:

[Agriculture Chair] Lucas won support from top GOP leaders, including Boehner; Majority Leader Cantor, R-Va.; and Whip Kevin McCarthy, R-Calif. However, the bill – which would have cut food stamps by $20.5 billion over the next 10 years – just didn't cut enough out of farm and nutrition programs for lawmakers aligned with the Tea Party, including Huelskamp and Stutzman, as well as Michele Bachmann, R-Minn.; Paul Broun, R-Ga.; and Steve Stockman, R-Texas.

They all voted "no" on final passage, which meant these "reformers" basically got nothing in terms of reforms. Without passage of a new farm bill, there would be zero cuts in food stamps, and direct payments would continue.

So what would it take to persuade those 62 Republican lawmakers to vote for passage of the farm bill? In some cases, the perfect seemed to be the enemy of the good. (Wyant 2017)[11]

Their desire for their perfect bill continued to be the enemy of getting more of what they wanted when the conference report came to a vote. As in prior versions of the bill, many Tea Party Republicans, including Michelle Bachmann (leader of the House Tea Party Caucus) voted against the conference report because it failed to make deep enough cuts to food stamps and agriculture subsidies. The final vote was 162 yeas and 63 nays within the Republican Party.

Similarly, the 2011 partisan standoff over raising the federal debt ceiling and cutting government spending resulted in a compromise bill. In the final bill (S. 365), both sides got some of what they wanted, but neither side got everything. Tea Party Republicans, for example, had changed the terms of the debate in Congress to focus on debt reduction. At the same time, they did not get all of what they wanted because the final deal did too little to reduce the deficit and because Congress did not have to pass a balanced-budget amendment before raising the debt limit ("Default Avoided at Eleventh Hour" 2011). Liberal Democrats were also unhappy with the final bill because the measure did not impose any new taxes on the rich and would include cuts to entitlement programs if the across-the-board cuts of sequestration went into effect ("Default

---

[11] 63 Republican legislators voted against the bill. The number 62 referenced here is a possible typo.

Avoided at Eleventh Hour" 2011). Ultimately, 174 Republicans supported the bill, while 66 voted against it. These examples highlight that the votes we study include compromises where neither side got everything they wanted and that legislators recognized this feature of the legislation.

Measuring Tea Party Attachment

The measure of Tea Party attachment in the district comes from the Cooperative Congressional Election Study (CCES) in waves conducted in 2010, 2012, and 2014. The CCES is a large-scale, collaborative survey that goes to tens of thousands of Americans during the Congressional elections every two years (Ansolabehere 2012; Ansolabehere and Schaffner 2013; Schaffner and Ansolabehere 2015). In the three waves used here, respondents were asked about their Tea Party attachment:

What is your view of the Tea Party movement; would you say it is very positive, somewhat positive, neutral, somewhat negative, or very negative, or don't you know enough about the Tea Party movement to say?

The independent variable for the analysis is the proportion of voters in the district who said that they had a positive view (either very positive or somewhat positive) of the Tea Party. Because Tea Party identifiers are more likely to support Tea Party candidates in primary elections (Karpowitz et al. 2011), this measure captures voters who might punish lawmakers for compromising by voting for a Tea Party challenger.

Controls

Legislators may reject compromise bills not just because they fear retribution for the compromise from Tea Party-aligned voters, but because their voters have more extreme conservative preferences and they are responsive to those preferences. Yet we seek to test the claim that the retribution for compromise is a driving force behind legislators' rejection of compromise proposals, above and beyond voters' desires for conservative policies. We control for the average ideology of strong Republican identifiers in the district to make sure that the Tea Party measure is not confounded with the ideological extremity of the primary voters. The average ideology of strong Republicans is calculated using an ideological self-placement question on a seven-point scale, where increasing values

TABLE 4.5. *Characteristics of Republican incumbents' constituents*

District Characteristic	Mean	Standard Deviation
Proportion with Positive View of Tea Party	0.28	0.064
Mean Ideology of Strong Republicans	6.2	0.20
Mean Voter Ideology	4.5	0.30
District Policy Preferences (Tausanovitch and Warshaw)	0.18	0.21

Notes: Data from the 2010, 2012, and 2014 Cooperative Congressional Elections Studies (Ansolabehere 2012; Ansolabehere and Schaffner 2013; Schaffner and Ansolabehere 2015), and from Tausanovitch and Warshaw (2013).

indicate greater levels of conservatism.[12] Controlling for the average ideology of strong Republicans in the district means that the Tea Party attachment variable detects the effect of the Tea Party above and beyond the average ideology of strong partisans in the district.

Similarly, we control for the average ideology of all voters in the district. Elections give politicians incentives to be responsive to both their primary and general electorate. We thus hold constant the average ideology of the general electorate, using the same ideology measure used above (but taking the average for all respondents in the district). As a robustness check, we also run a model where we use the estimate of district preferences from Tausanovitch and Warshaw (2013). We include this analysis to see if the result is robust to different ways of capturing the preferences of the general electorate. Table 4.5 gives the mean and standard deviation for Tea Party attachment and the control variables. Finally, the models include fixed effects for Congress to account for any idiosyncratic factors associated with the dynamics during each Congress.

Predicting Rejection of Compromise with District Tea Party Support

Results from a linear probability model with fixed effects by Congress and standard errors clustered by legislator (Table 4.6) show that increased Tea Party attachment among constituents is associated with a reduced likelihood of legislators voting for the compromise

[12] How would you rate each of the following individuals and groups? Yourself (Options: Very Liberal, Liberal, Somewhat Liberal, Middle of the Road, Somewhat Conservative, Conservative, Very Conservative).

TABLE 4.6. *Tea Party identifiers as predictors of compromise*

Dependent Variable = Vote Yes	(1)	(2)
Proportion with Positive View of Tea Party	−0.69*	−0.86*
	(0.25)	(0.22)
Mean Ideology of Strong Republicans	−0.036	−0.032
	(0.054)	(0.053)
Mean Voter Ideology	−0.18*	
	(0.054)	
District Policy Preferences (Tausanovitch and Warshaw)		−0.25*
		(0.069)
113th Congress	−0.074*	−0.059*
	(0.017)	(0.020)
114th Congress	−0.11*	−0.097*
	(0.020)	(0.022)
Intercept	1.9*	1.16*
	(0.36)	(0.31)
N	7,214	7,214
R-Squared	0.033	0.033

Note: Models estimated using OLS regression. The dependent variable is an indicator equal to one if the Republican legislator voted yes on the roll call vote. Standard errors clustered by legislator shown in parentheses.
*$p < 0.05$ (two-sided).

proposal. Substantively, a one standard deviation increase in Tea Party attachment (a 6.4% increase in people who say they have a very strong attachment to the Tea Party) is associated with a 4.6–5.3 percentage point decrease in the likelihood that a legislator will vote in favor of the compromise legislation ($p = 0.005$, two-sided). The more Tea Party voters there were in the district, the more likely the member of Congress was to vote against compromise legislation. These results hold even when controlling for the ideology of the primary and general electorates. The threat of punishment by primary voters does not just affect state legislators' survey responses about compromise. It also negatively affects the willingness of members of Congress to vote for compromises on important issues.

DISCUSSION

Legislators believe that primary voters are much more likely to punish them for compromising than general election voters or donors. This fear of punishment by primary voters leads many legislators to reject compromise. For example, members of Congress whose voters expressed greater approval of the Tea Party were more likely to vote no on key votes that required bipartisan compromises.

What is behind this fear of retribution for compromise from primary voters? Certainly some of the high profile instances of primary challenges, including those from the Tea Party, contribute to legislators' perceptions. In open-ended questions in the NCSL survey, 43% of respondents said that they could name a time when a legislator had lost their seat because they voted for a compromise. The respondents mentioned legislators who had lost their seats because of compromise votes for Medicaid expansion and other state-level health care reforms, budget bills, and transportation funding, among others. Some specifically noted challenges in the primary (especially on the right), going so far as to name state legislators and members of Congress who had lost in primary elections. Many legislators are aware of specific instances where their colleagues lost a seat because of compromise. As a result, legislators may believe they have reason to fear primary voter punishment for compromise as well.

A high-profile case when legislators did compromise in 2013 high-lights how legislators' fear of primary voters can be a barrier to compromise, but that some legislators are willing to take the risk if they think they can overcome the punishment. At that time, Susan Collins (R-ME), Lisa Murkowski (R-AK), and Kelly Ayotte (R-NH) brokered a compromise proposal that unlinked defunding Obamacare from funding the government to end a 16-day government shutdown.[13] They encouraged their fellow Republicans to extend the debt ceiling and reopen the government while maintaining automatic across-the-board cuts (sequestrations). The compromise passed with 87 House Republicans voting yea and 144 voting nay. Ironically, it may have been Senator Murkowski's own primary loss to a Tea Party candidate in 2010 that emboldened her to advocate for the compromise. After losing in her primary election in 2010, Murkowski went on to win the general election as a write-in candidate. Because she believed she could overcome voter punishment in the primary again, she may have been less worried than other Republicans. She told the *New York Times*, "I probably will have retribution in my state. That's fine. That doesn't bother me at all. If there is backlash, hey, that's what goes on in D.C., but in the meantime there is a government that is shut down. There are people who are really hurting" (Weisman

---

[13] This legislation is included in the previous analysis of compromise votes in Congress and Tea Party support in the district.

and Steinhauer 2013). Indeed, Senator Murkowski's past experience had made it clear that a part of the primary electorate was willing to punish, but unlike most legislators, she knew she could overcome this punishment in the primary and win a general election. Yet, not all legislators have the experience of overcoming punishment, and many may reject compromise when they worry about retribution from the primary electorate.

Media coverage that paints compromise in a negative light may magnify the perceived risks of compromising and the likelihood of facing a primary challenger from the far left or far right. In the 2017 survey at the NCSL Summit, we asked the legislators how various media outlets covered compromise. The majority of legislators (60%) thought that cable news outlets like MSNBC and Fox News portrayed legislative compromises in a negative light, while only 12% of legislators thought that these outlets portrayed it in a positive light. While legislators thought that national network news, major newspapers, and the local media were more neutral in their presentation, enough likely primary voters watch news like MSNBC and Fox to give legislators pause when considering compromise.

A lingering question, however, is whether this fear of voter retribution is accurate. Legislators' perceptions of constituency opinion are often inaccurate (e.g., Broockman and Skovron 2018). Are legislators correctly inferring how voters view compromise? During the open-ended portion of our survey, one legislator argued that "compromise is increasingly being viewed as a violation of principals, so people (including legislators) may be more averse to it" (2017 NCSL Attendee 48). Do voters see compromise this way? Or, are legislators overestimating the opposition to compromise, even among subsets of primary voters? It is possible that the presence of even a small number of activists who oppose compromise affects legislators' perceptions of their broader constituency, leading them to believe this position is much more widely held than it is (Karol 2015). One legislator suggested that things might not be as bad as legislators think. While agreeing that legislators reject compromises because of fear of voter punishment, this legislator noted that "[other legislators] feel like they experience it worse than they do" (2017 NCSL Attendee 19). Chapter 5 addresses this assessment by surveying Americans about their views on compromise and examining whether likely primary voters will punish legislators if they compromise.

5

Voter Punishment Is Rare but Real

> Voters seem to say they want [compromise] until we actually do it. Then,
> they don't like it because the idea of it is better than the reality.
>
> 2017 NCSL Attendee 82

In 2017, Illinois lawmakers entered a third year of stalemate over the
budget. Without a budget for the previous two years, the state's public
universities had suffered and risked losing their accreditation, social service providers had closed their doors, layoffs of road construction crews
were imminent, and legislators faced the risk that the state's credit rating would be downgraded to junk status (Garcia and Geiger 2017). As
the deadline loomed, Democratic legislators pushed forward a balanced
budget compromise that included an increase in the state income tax.
Democratic House Speaker Michael Madigan called the budget bill "a
crucial step toward reaching a compromise that ends the budget crisis
by passing a fully funded state budget in a bipartisan way" (Garcia and
Geiger 2017). The bill received support from 72 out of 118 members in
the House, including more than a dozen Republicans. In the Senate, the
support of one Republican gave the Senate Democrats the numbers to
override Republican Governor Bruce Rauner's veto. The senator who
compromised, Dale Righter, said he would like to have seen more spending reductions, "but in a Democrat-majority legislature, this is as good
as we can get" (Associated Press 2017).

The Republicans in both chambers who broke with their party to support the compromise knew that doing so involved electoral risks. This
was a high-profile issue and their votes were pivotal in the bill's passage.
"For me right here today, right here, right now, this is a sword that I'm

willing to die on," said Republican Michael Unes. "And if it costs me my seat, so be it" (Garcia and Geiger 2017). Republican Terri Bryant, a fiscal conservative who hates tax increases but acknowledged the necessity of the state paying its bills to small businesses, said that she expected to face a primary challenger because of her vote (Garcia and Geiger 2017). She did. Paul Jacobs made Bryant's budget vote a central issue in his campaign for the nomination in 2018 and captured 45% of the vote (Richard 2018).

Bryant's retention of the nomination and her seat notwithstanding, Republicans seemed right to worry that supporting this budget compromise would lead to punishment from their base. Conservative groups mobilized voters to send the Republican legislators a strong message of opposition to this compromise. The Illinois Policy Institute, for example, had warned its subscribers that House Republican floor leader Steven Andersson and other Republicans might vote with the Democrats on the compromise. Somehow the cellphone numbers of Andersson and others who voted for the tax bill were distributed publicly.[1] Republican legislators who compromised subsequently received a barrage of angry and even threatening communications from constituents. One legislator was told he'd be "hanging from a tree" and another was told "You are selling your soul to the devil" (Korecki 2017).

Ultimately, four Republicans who supported the tax hike opted not to run again, and many of the remaining members faced primary challengers who were supported by conservative groups that expressed a desire for principles over compromise (Pearson 2018). For instance, conservative operative Dan Proft's Liberty Principles PAC spent more than $1.2 million in the GOP primary to unseat Jim Durkin, the Republican leader he blamed for failing to keep Republicans unified in opposition to the budget compromise. This pushback was evident even immediately after the vote, when Steven Andersson was deposed as the House Republican floor leader. He then announced that he would not seek reelection in 2018, noting the pressure to avoid working toward compromises. As he explained in a television interview, "I consider myself a moderate Republican, which means I tend to cross the aisle a lot, and it becomes increasingly difficult around here to function in that role" (Vinicky 2017).

---

[1] While some blamed the Illinois Policy Institute, the Institute denied being behind it (Korecki 2017).

The example of cap and trade legislation in California – a story referenced in Chapter 1 – also highlights the pressure legislators can face to not compromise. In July 2017, California lawmakers voted to renew the state's cap and trade program to reduce emissions of the gases that contribute to climate change. The final bill offered tax credits to manufacturers and power providers and facilitated a 40% cut in greenhouse gas emissions from 1990 levels by 2030 (Washington Post Editorial Board 2017). At the time, the editorial board of the *Sacramento Bee* described the bill as a compromise in which "no one gets everything, and everyone gets something. That's called compromise. It's how reasonable policy gets done" (Sacramento Bee Editorial Board 2017).

The compromise nature of the bill caused a split in both parties. On the Democratic side, Democratic Assembly Member Limón opposed it because she thought the tax credits meant that it did not go far enough in making oil and utility companies pay the costs (Welsh 2017). On the Republican side, many prominent Republicans outside the legislature publicly supported the bill, including former California Governors Arnold Schwarzenegger and Pete Wilson and former Secretary of State George Shultz. However, these politicians were retired and no longer worried about retribution from the electorate. By contrast, Republicans in the legislature did have to worry about voter retribution and most of them voted against the bill. Among the 55 yes votes in the Assembly, only 7 were Republicans. The Republican Party leader, Assembly Member Chad Mayes, who voted for the compromise legislation, lost his party leadership position to a member who voted against the cap and trade legislation (McGreevy 2017). And at a Tea Party meeting the month after the vote, former Assembly Member Tim Donnely called for Republicans in California to unseat Mayes in the June primary with a Tea Party candidate (Willon 2017). While this did not come to pass, such threats can restrain compromise.

These examples suggest that legislators may be right to worry that they can face a serious primary challenge if they compromise. Some members, particularly where primary threats are more serious than general election risks, may fear retribution for compromising. But how widespread is voter opposition to compromise? Does the public generally favor or oppose compromise? And what about the subsets of the public who are likely to vote in primary elections – the engaged, ideological, and strong partisans? Do these primary voters have a clear preference for legislators rejecting compromise, and do they punish legislators who support compromise?

This chapter presents the results of a survey experiment that assesses whether voters punish or reward legislators who compromise. Although Chapter 4 shows that legislators are most concerned about voters in the primary election, we look at the behavior of all voters and then separately at the behavior of primary voters to examine whether these electorates actually differ in their response to compromise.

The survey experiment aligns with the vignette presented to state legislators in Chapter 4, allowing us to examine voter opinion in parallel with legislators' perceptions. We focus on the most likely case of voter punishment for compromise – when their legislator's vote is consequential and difficult. While most voters value compromise, the subset of co-partisan primary voters in the study who oppose the specific compromise punish legislators for compromising. This set of voters is not likely to be a majority of all voters, but they are substantial enough to worry legislators, particularly given that these subsets of voters may be more likely to organize. Moreover, legislators face many possible compromise votes, which means they may face punishment from many such subsets of voters that collectively represent a sizable fraction of their primary electorate.

PUBLIC OPINION ON COMPROMISE

Public opinion polls show that the public generally professes to like compromise. In 2014, for example, 61% of respondents in a Pew poll indicated that "I like elected officials who make compromises with people they disagree with" came closer to their views than "I like elected officials who stick to their positions" (Pew 2014a). This generic form of question about compromise regularly yields high levels of support for legislators who compromise. A set of questions in the 2012 American National Election Study (ANES) showed even higher support for generic compromise: 68% of respondents preferred a president who "compromises to get things done" (DeBell et al. 2012). Only 32% of respondents said they preferred a President who would "stick to principles no matter what." The numbers were comparable when they were asked about their representatives in Congress. And again in the 2016 ANES, support for compromise from a government official was 65% (Hutchings et al. 2017). In all cases, supermajorities of the public say they want leaders to compromise.

The existing scholarly studies offer a mixed perspective on public opposition to compromise, but generally suggest that compromising is a net benefit for legislators' reelection prospects (for a review, see Wolak 2017b).

For example, studies show that the public does not want legislators to always vote with the party (Carson et al. 2010; Koger and Lebo 2017) and prefers policy compromise over legislative inaction (Flynn and Harbridge 2016; Bauer et al. 2017). However, the public also responds favorably to ideological consistency in members' voting (Koger and Lebo 2017) and prefers legislative victories for their side over bipartisan compromise (Harbridge et al. 2014). With these caveats in mind, the literature generally concludes that legislators stand to benefit from compromise more than they stand to lose.

How can this be reconciled with legislators' apparent concern about voter punishment in primaries? Are legislators needlessly worrying? Perhaps not. Legislators might not take these polls showing general support for compromise at face value because the questions are so abstract, because they do not think the national numbers represent their district's preferences on compromise, or because the overall support for compromise masks opposition from a subset of voters in the primaries who punish compromise.

The compromise questions referenced above are notably abstract, without context about policy or parties. Pundits have noted that preferences for compromise in general may not map onto preferences for compromise on specific issues on which voters have strong views – where compromise is seen as capitulation or betrayal (Bullock 2016). As the NCSL attendee quoted at the beginning of this chapter put it, "the idea of [compromise] is better than the reality" (2017 NCSL Attendee 82). Compromise in the abstract may be more appealing than in a policy context where it is clear what your side gives up to achieve the deal. And preferences for compromise in general may not play out when partisanship comes into play, such as when a compromise involves a legislator breaking with her party. Even people who express a preference for bipartisanship in the abstract prefer legislation that reflects a victory for their party when the details of the policy and agreement are noted (Harbridge et al. 2014).

Along these lines, the same Pew (2014a) study described above asked the following question:

Thinking about how Barack Obama and Republican leaders should address the most important issues facing the country. Imagine a scale from zero to 100 where 100 means Republican leaders get everything they want and Obama gets nothing he wants, and zero means Obama gets everything and Republican leaders get nothing. Where on this scale from zero to 100 do you think they should end up?

Unlike the generic compromise question discussed above, this question describes compromise as being carried out by partisan teams. The content of the policy is still abstract, but the partisan nature of the potential compromise is made explicit. When described this way, support for compromise is lower. In this case, only half of respondents (52%) say that the two sides should meet in the middle at 50, as opposed to the more than 60% who support compromise when the generic non-partisan question is asked.

Both policy and partisan concerns, rather than a generic concern about compromise, appear to be reflected in the anger at Republicans who supported the Illinois budget compromise. Republican voters saw support for the compromise as a "partisan betrayal" (Korecki 2017) and saw the Republicans as accepting a loss (the large tax increase) without sufficient victories to justify it (spending cuts or a property tax freeze).

Moreover, a concern that key voters may respond negatively to specific compromises may motivate legislators to oppose compromise on floor votes despite the generic support for it in the public. Even when polls show sizable majorities supporting compromise, a subset of voters – especially those who form key parts of a legislator's primary constituency, like voters with more extreme ideology, strong partisans, donors, and those who support ideologically rigid groups – may oppose compromise. Previous chapters showed that legislators are particularly concerned about the individuals who vote in primaries. Republicans especially worry that they will lose in the primary election, with 39% of state legislators who won in 2016 saying they would worry more about losing in 2018 in a primary rather than a general election. Still, almost 20% of Democrats share this sense that they are more vulnerable in the primary election (Skovron 2018). These numbers are striking given the small fraction of incumbents who actually lose in a primary election and suggest that legislators are attuned to the risks of upsetting the primary electorate. If key groups within the legislator's primary electorate oppose compromise, a desire for compromise from the public at large may not be enough to override the subgroup's opposition, especially if it comes from co-partisans.

Primary voters are more likely to have stronger ideological positions and stronger partisan attachments that may lead them to oppose compromise. Among the public, most Americans place themselves near the middle of the ideological spectrum (Fiorina et al. 2005). "Real liberals and real conservatives are found in impressive numbers only among the comparatively few who are deeply and seriously engaged in political life"

(Kinder and Kalmoe 2017, 7). But, even if committed ideologues are not the norm among the general population, they are important to members' reelection efforts. These strongly ideological voters, the very ones who are also likely to be politically involved primary voters, may simply be warier of compromise because they have strong views and have less that they are willing to give up. These voters' partisan attachments may also be an obstacle to compromise. Partisanship is a durable and important political identity (Campbell et al. 1960; Green et al. 2002) and partisanship may be a central part of social identity (Klar 2013; Mason 2015). When partisanship is a strong social identity, people exhibit more favoritism toward their party and derogation toward the other party (Greene 2004; Mason 2013).[2] This strong sense of party attachment might cause some voters to oppose compromise because they simply do not want to work with the other side. Primary voters are likely to exhibit these strong levels of party attachment and therefore may be more likely to oppose compromise.

The Pew and ANES data verify that some subgroups are less supportive of compromise. Table 5.1 shows the support for compromise among all respondents and a few key subgroups in the population: those who self-identified as very liberal or very conservative, as strong partisans, as donors, and as Tea Party supporters. Each column corresponds to one of the measures of compromise mentioned earlier in the chapter.

Across all ways of asking about compromise, support for compromise is substantially lower among very liberal or very conservative respondents and among Tea Party supporters compared to the general public. For example, the data from Pew (column 1) show that generic support for legislators who compromise drops from 61% overall to less than a majority for the very liberal or very conservative (46%) and Tea Party supporters (37%). Majorities of strong partisans and donors continue to express support for legislators who compromise.[3] In the ANES data,

---

[2] Partisanship need not be central for all members of the public. Some citizens may be ambivalent partisans, recognizing some of the weaknesses of their own party's policies and performance and some of the strengths of the opposing party (Lavine et al. 2012).

[3] In the 2014 Pew data, "donor" describes someone who contributed money to a candidate running for public office or to a group working to elect a candidate. Similarly, in the 2012 ANES, "donor" describes someone who gave to a candidate running for office, a political party, or any other groups that supported or opposed them. In the 2016 ANES, "donor" describes someone who gave money to a social or political organization. If a question specifically focusing on donating money to a political campaign is used, 73% of donors favor compromise.

TABLE 5.1. *Support for compromise in Pew and ANES among subgroups*

	Pew Compromise vs. Stick to Positions	ANES 2012 President Compromise vs. Stick to Principles	ANES 2012 Congress Compromise vs. Stick to Principles	ANES 2016 Government Official Compromise	*Pew* Negotiation 50-50 Split
Percent who prefer compromise among…					
All respondents	61%	68%	69%	65%	52%
Very liberal/very conservative	46%	52%	56%	51%	32%
Strong partisans	61%	66%	68%	62%	40%
Donors	67%	69%	71%	74%	44%
Tea Party supporters	37%	53%	49%	N/A	42%

Note: Calculations by the authors from the 2014 Pew survey (2014a) and the 2012 and 2016 American National Election Studies (DeBell et al. 2012; Hutchings et al. 2017). Note that ideology is a five-point scale in the Pew data and a seven-point scale in the ANES data.

the patterns largely follow those of the abstract compromise question in Pew. Support for compromise is substantially lower among ideologues and Tea Party supporters, whether the government official is generic, the president, or a member of Congress.

As noted above, survey respondents show lower support for compromise when researchers pose the question as a negotiation between two partisan groups than when they discuss it in the abstract. Among all respondents, just over half (52%) said that the two sides should meet in the middle at 50. As with compromise in the generic form, support for this more concrete partisan compromise is lower among subgroups of the electorate. Among ideologues, only a third (32%) favor an even compromise. Majorities of strong partisans, campaign donors, and Tea Party supporters also oppose compromise with the other party, suggesting that legislators may be right that these electorally important subgroups of primary voters oppose compromises made with the opposing party.

However, even if these abstract questions accurately capture a preference among likely primary voters for legislators to stick to their principles and not compromise, this opposition to compromise may not manifest in punishment. Voters may still vote for their incumbent representative even when they are frustrated that the incumbent supported a compromise proposal. If voters are not willing to withhold their votes from incumbents who compromise, then politicians may still have electoral incentives to pursue and support compromises. When specific policies are being negotiated, do these key voters disapprove of *and* vote against incumbents who compromise? We examine this question by turning to a survey experiment.

ASSESSING WHETHER VOTERS PUNISH COMPROMISE

State legislators who worry about voter retribution are more likely to reject a half-loaf compromise than those who do not. When asked how voters would like a member of Congress to vote on a compromise, state legislators distinguished between primary and general election voters. They overwhelmingly said that primary voters would want the member to vote no on the compromise and kill the bill, while general election voters would want the member to vote yes to pass the compromise (see Chapter 4). In December 2017, we surveyed a representative sample of 2,029 Americans about their preferences for compromise in a way that mirrors the question we had posed to legislators. The survey, fielded to members of the Qualtrics panel, was balanced to be representative of the national population in terms of age, gender, ethnicity/race, and region.

Now we are going to ask you about a bill that was closely contested and how your Senator's action on that bill affects your approval of them.

Suppose that Democrats and Republicans in Congress battled over the issue of {securing America's energy}. After a great deal of disagreement and negotiation by Democrats and Republicans over the {extent of investment in green energy}, they voted on a bill that contained about half of the {investment in green energy} that [Democrats like Michael Bennet (CO)] wanted.]

Senator [Bennet], your Senator, was one of only a few from their party who voted [FOR/AGAINST] this compromise bill. Ultimately, the bill [PASSED/FAILED] by just one vote.

FIGURE 5.1. Vignette to assess public reactions to compromise when it is most consequential.
Note: The vignette above provides an example of the text that a Colorado resident assigned to energy policy and randomly assigned to Senator Michael Bennet (D-CO) would have seen. We use Senator Michael Bennet as an example throughout this section. Within the survey experiment, this name reflected the assigned senator (on the basis of state), as indicated by the square brackets. A Colorado respondent assigned to Republican Senator Cory Gardner would have been told that the bill focused on the expansion of oil and gas production in America (as indicated by the curly brackets) and that the bill contained about half of the expansion that Republicans like Cory Gardner wanted. Once the assignment to the senator voting for or against the compromise was complete, the passage or failure of the bill was made consistent with that stance. More generally, the text given in brackets varied randomly across legislators. The text given in curly brackets was taken or calculated from legislators' prior answers or from current policy.

The survey included a vignette (Figure 5.1) that described a bill that was closely contested between the parties and where the final proposal included half of the policy change that their senator and others in his or her party wanted. It stated that the majority of the senator's party would oppose the bill and that the senator's vote was likely to be pivotal. The experiment randomized whether the senator voted for or against the compromise.

The experimental vignette provides four key benefits. First, the vignette provides a most-likely case scenario for finding punishment by studying compromise when it is most difficult and consequential – when others in the senator's party are opposing the bill and when the senator's vote will be pivotal to whether the legislation passes. This most-likely case design allows us to test whether there is a reason for legislators to be afraid; if voters are not punishing in this scenario, they are likely not punishing in less consequential and less difficult situations either. Because this test is designed to find the most likely scenarios for voter punishment, these results likely provide an upper bound on the extent of punishment for compromise. Second, by presenting a similar vignette to the one we presented to legislators (as described in Chapter 4), we provide a comparison between legislators' perceptions and voters' intended actions. In Chapter 4, we asked legislators about their voters and now we ask voters about their legislators. Third, the vignette directly assesses whether voters punish members for compromising, holding constant other elements of the compromise. As a result, we can compare the average evaluation of the senator when she compromises and when she does not compromise to assess whether the senator is rewarded or punished for compromising. We can then make the same assessment for whether respondents would vote for or against the legislator, the most direct test of punishment. Fourth, the vignette asks voters about their own senator, which allows us to focus on how actual constituents respond to legislative compromise within a realistic context. To enhance the validity of the inferences from the study, respondents reported their state and were randomly assigned, with equal probability, to one of the two senators from their state.[4]

Prior to reading the vignette, respondents were asked about their party identification to determine whether they were co-partisans of their assigned senator. The intuition of whether a voter is likely to punish a legislator who supports compromise is very different depending on whether the voter and the legislator are from the same party. When people are evaluating members of the opposing party, bipartisanship and compromise seem to improve evaluations of legislators (Paris 2017). By contrast, bipartisanship and compromise does less to improve citizens' evaluations of legislators of their own party (Bauer et al. 2017), and in some cases, bipartisanship has a negative impact on evaluations of co-partisan legislators (Harbridge and Malhotra 2011). Consistent with this asymmetric party effect, Ditto and Mastronarde (2009) found that people expressed more positive views of political mavericks when they were described generally than when prompted to consider a maverick of their own political party. We compare the behavior of opposing partisans and co-partisans and then consider subsets of co-partisan voters who might be most likely to punish – self-identified primary voters, voters with characteristics that might correlate with greater political engagement and primary activism, and voters who oppose compromise.

---

[4] Senators who identified as Independent (e.g., Bernie Sanders of Vermont) and those who had announced their retirement at the time we were fielding the survey (e.g., Bob Corker, Luther Strange, Jeff Flake, and Al Franken) were excluded, and respondents from those states were assigned to the other incumbent senator.

In the study, respondents were asked what approach or means they would use to deal with the following four issues: creating new jobs, making the United States energy secure, balancing the budget, and securing Social Security and Medicare.⁵ There were three options for how to approach each issue: a conservative or Republican approach, a liberal or Democratic approach, and a mix of both the conservative and the liberal approach. For example, respondents were asked whether they preferred to secure Social Security and Medicare via increased taxes, decreased benefits, or a combination of both strategies.⁶

Where possible, respondents were randomly assigned to a vignette that focused on an issue where they took a position on what strategy to use (as opposed to using a combination of the two strategies).⁷ In addition, the self-identified partisans in the sample were assigned to an issue on which they took a party-consistent stance if possible.⁸ That is, if the respondent identified with the Democratic Party, she would be assigned to one of the issues where she preferred the liberal approach to solving the problem. If the respondent identified with the Republican Party, she would be assigned to an issue on which she preferred the conservative approach.⁹ For example, a respondent who identified as a Democrat and

---

⁵ These are issues that the group No Labels has indicated are ripe for agreement in principle. A Democrat or a Republican could endorse these goals even if he or she might disagree on the means for achieving the goal.

⁶ Respondents asked about the goal of creating new jobs were offered, "The government should create new jobs by providing tax incentives to companies in order to hire new workers," "The government should create new jobs by expanding government activities that hire new employees," or a combination. Respondents asked about energy security were offered "The government should secure America's energy future by easing regulations in order to expand oil and gas production in America," "The government should secure America's energy future by investing in green energy," or a combination. Respondents asked about balancing the budget were offered "The government should balance the budget by cutting spending on social programs," "The government should balance the budget by increasing taxes," or a combination.

⁷ If a respondent chose the combination of strategies on all four issues, the respondent was randomly assigned to one of the issues for the vignette.

⁸ If the respondent was an Independent, she was randomly assigned to an issue where she had chosen a preferred means on the issue. If the respondent was a partisan and did not take any party-consistent stances or was an Independent and did not choose a preferred means, she was randomly assigned an issue.

⁹ Of the 1,631 partisans in the sample, 1,395 took a party-consistent position (and just 236 did not). Of the 282 Independents in the sample, 266 took a position on the means (and only 16 did not). All respondents are included in the analysis. However, the results are the same when limited to partisans who took party-consistent positions and Independents who took a clear position on the means.

chose increased taxes to secure Social Security and Medicare might be
assigned to that issue or another on which she also chose the liberal
policy tool. A respondent who identified as a Democrat but chose cutting benefits to secure Social Security and Medicare would be assigned
to a different issue on which she chose a party-consistent approach. In
all cases, the compromise offered in the vignette focused on the party-
aligned goal of the senator for the issue to which the respondent was
assigned.

This assignment strategy ensures that the compromise offered in the
vignette is viewed as a half-loaf offer for co-partisans with party-consistent
stances. The vignette focused on a simple, unidimensional compromise.
That single issue focus ensures that co-partisans of the assigned senator
who took a party-consistent stance are getting some (though not all) of
what they want in the compromise. It is less clear whether the compromise bill offered to opposing party senators would be seen as a half-loaf
offer for an opposing partisan voter or for a co-partisan voter who takes
a party-inconsistent stance. Voters in the opposing party might oppose
their senator's party-consistent support for compromise because it gives
the senator part of what she wanted (which was different from what the
voter wanted). Or voters in the opposing party might view the compromise as giving them a policy success because the senator from the opposing party did not get everything she wanted. In either case, however, the
voter may not see compromise as a half-loaf offer relative to the status
quo. In the analyses that follow, we begin with all respondents and then
focus on co-partisans.

Figure 5.1 shows an example of the vignette for a respondent
from Colorado who was assigned to the issue of energy policy and
to Democratic Senator Michael Bennet. The vignette experimentally
manipulates whether the senator voted for the compromise.

After reading the vignette, respondents were asked about three measures of support for the senator they had read about: approval, whether
the respondent would vote for the senator in the general election, and
(for co-partisans) whether the respondent would vote for the senator in
the primary election. Directly following the vignette that randomized
whether the senator had voted for the compromise, we asked respondents to indicate whether they approve or disapprove of the job that
the senator is doing. The response options ranged from strongly disapprove (1) to strongly approve (6) on a six-point scale. The next two measures also assess punishment but move from approval to vote intention.
For Democratic respondents in Colorado, for example, we asked them,

"If the *primary* election for the Senate seat held by Senator Bennet were held today, would you vote for Senator Bennet?" The response options were yes (1) or no (0). All respondents then saw a question about vote intention in the *general* election. For co-partisans, we include both the primary and general election vote intention measures because voters might punish co-partisan senators in the primary – where the alternative may be a co-partisan senator who is committed to not compromising – but might not punish in the general election – where the alternative is a challenger from the opposing party.

On each measure, we examine the effect of the senator compromising relative to not compromising using OLS regression, which is equivalent to measuring the difference in means. If voters reward legislators for compromising, compromising should have a positive effect on approval and vote choice. If voters punish legislators for compromising, compromising should have a negative effect on approval and vote choice. The analysis that follows begins by looking at respondents as a whole and then drills down into specific subsets of potential voters: co-partisans, likely primary voters, and those who oppose the specific compromise. We test whether there are any identifiable groups in the population who punish compromise.

ANALYZING VOTER RESPONSES TO COMPROMISE

Voters Overall and by Partisan Subgroups

Initial analyses suggest that senators are rewarded for compromising. Among all respondents, those told that their senator supported the compromise approve of their senator by half a point (0.47; $p < 0.001$, two-sided) more than those told that their senator voted against the compromise. On a scale that ranges from 1 to 6, half a point is a substantial increase in approval. Rather than being punished for compromise, senators are rewarded, at least when looking at the response from all voters.

Legislators are sophisticated in their assessment of the electorate and know that they do not need to win the support of every voter in the state or district. They recognize an outsized need to appeal to co-partisans and independents (Fenno 1978; Butler 2009). Moreover, they note that their worries about voter punishment stem mainly from the primary election (see Chapter 4), which is predominantly co-partisans (Sides et al. 2018).

The survey experiment here allows us to assess whether co-partisans, independents, and partisans from the other party behave differently when a senator compromises.

Separating the participants by the major partisan groups – co-partisans, Independents, and opposing partisans – does not reveal a partisan group that punishes. As shown in Figure 5.2 (upper panel), being told that their senator supported a compromise raises levels of approval among each partisan subgroup. Although the increase among Independents is smaller

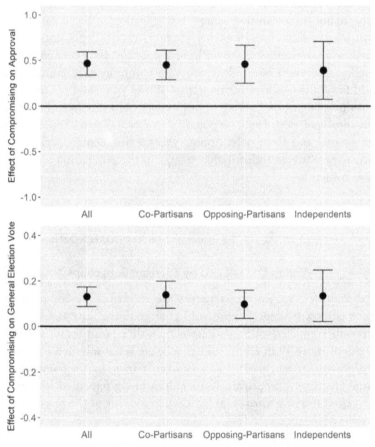

FIGURE 5.2. All partisan groups and subgroups approve more of senators who compromise and are more likely to vote for senators who compromise in the general election.
Note: Effect of compromising is measured as the difference between the average response in the compromise and no compromise conditions. Bars represent 95% confidence intervals.

(0.39) than the other subgroups, it is still positive (and does not differ significantly from the positive effect observed among other subgroups). Moreover, all three partisan subgroups are more likely to report that they would vote for a compromising senator in the general election than an uncompromising senator (see Figure 5.2 lower panel). Co-partisans (the only ones who were asked about the primary) are even significantly more likely to report they would vote for a compromising senator in the primary election. The increase in vote intention among co-partisans in the primary electorate was smaller in size (0.12; $p < 0.001$, two-sided) than the increases reported in Figure 5.2, but still significantly positive. In short, the initial results do not support the view that legislators will be punished for compromise in the general or primary election.

Likely Primary Voters

Legislators are specifically concerned that primary voters, or even a subset of primary voters, will punish them for compromising. Given that we find no punishment in terms of approval or votes among all co-partisans, we use various ways of capturing subsets of voters who might matter more in primary elections. We identify this subgroup most directly by asking for a self-report of whether they voted in the 2016 primary election.[10] Because punishment by even a subset of primary voters might be enough to put cautious politicians on notice, we also consider several other characteristics of respondents that might correlate with activism in the primary election – strength of party identification, extremity of ideology, being a campaign donor, and support for primary election-oriented groups (the Tea Party and Indivisible/ Resist). We limit this analysis to those who share the partisan identity of the senator to focus on those who would most likely be part of the senator's primary electorate.

The subgroup analyses show that these groups of voters generally reward senators who support compromise. Figure 5.3 reports these results, with the top half of the figure giving the results on approval and the bottom half giving the results on vote intention in the primary election. The results are similar for vote intention in the general election (not pictured).

---

[10] We follow the 2016 ANES in providing respondents with one option to indicate they are sure they voted in the election and several options that reflect alternatives for why they did not vote in the election, to reduce the extent of social desirability bias and the resulting overstatement of voting.

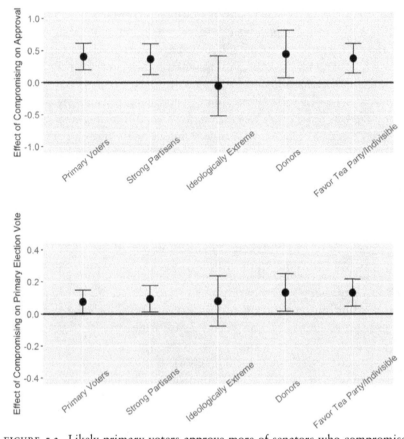

FIGURE 5.3. Likely primary voters approve more of senators who compromise and are more likely to vote for them in the primary election.
Note: Effect of compromising is measured as the difference between the average response in the compromise and no compromise conditions. Bars represent 95% confidence intervals.

For both outcomes, the majority of these subgroups are more likely to approve of and vote for the compromising senator. The one exception to this increased support for senators who compromise is among the most ideologically extreme respondents (those who are extremely liberal or extremely conservative). For this group there is no statistically significant difference in evaluations between those who are told that their senator supported the compromise and those who are told she opposed it. Despite worry about primary voters, even key subsets of likely primary voters are, on average, more supportive of senators who vote for compromise.

Voters Who Oppose Compromise

Is there a subset of voters who *penalize* a legislator for compromising? The results thus far suggest that legislators should not be worried about voter punishment in the general or primary election. However, even a small subset of voters can matter in an election and active, engaged, and angry primary voters can derail a legislator's campaign. So rather than seeking the average effect of compromising among subsets of voters as defined by their general political identities, we now analyze the subset of voters who either oppose compromise in general or oppose the specific compromise their senator voted on.

First, we ask whether voters who oppose compromise in general are likely to punish senators who vote for it. We measure the concept of opposition to compromise by respondents' responses to a question drawn from the national polls: "Would you prefer an elected official who compromises to get things done, or who sticks to his or her principles no matter what?"[11] We again restrict our analysis to voters who are their senator's co-partisans and to self-identified primary voters.

Figure 5.4 shows the effect of compromise on all three outcomes: approval, vote in the primary, and vote in the general election. Among co-partisan primary voters who say that they prefer a politician who sticks to her principles no matter what, compromise has no effect on approval. Compromise does not boost approval of senators among this subset of voters, but it does not hurt them either. In fact, compromise has a positive effect on these voters' intention to support their senator in the next election. In other words, even voters with a preference for legislators to stick to their principles in general are nonetheless, on average, more likely to vote for the senator when she supported the specific compromise.[12]

Second, we ask whether voters who oppose the specific compromise on the means for addressing this policy goal punish senators who vote

[11] Because this question has both the potential to prime respondents in their answer to the compromise vignette and to be affected by the treatment, we randomize whether this question is asked as the first or last question in the survey. Including a three-way interaction between the compromise treatment, preference for compromise, and whether the compromise question was asked at the beginning or the end of the survey indicates that question order does not affect the results.

[12] Results are similar among all co-partisans who oppose compromise (i.e., when co-partisans who do not report that they voted in the primary are included). Moreover, the effect of compromise among co-partisans who oppose compromise is indistinguishable from the effect of compromise among co-partisans who generally prefer compromises to get things done.

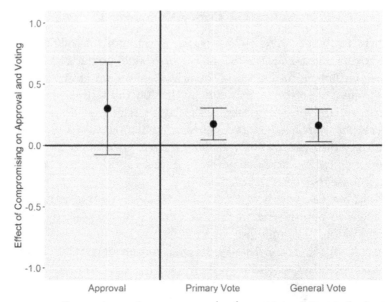

FIGURE 5.4. Co-partisan primary voters who do not want compromise in general do not punish senators who compromise.

Note: Effect of compromising is measured as the difference between the average response in the compromise and no compromise conditions. Bars represent 95% confidence intervals. The solid line between the dependent variables highlights that the scale of the first measure (approval) is different from the scale of the next two measures (vote intention). For approval, the dependent variable ranges from 1 (strongly disapprove) to 6 (strongly approve). For primary and general election vote, the dependent variable is a binary measure where voting for the member is a 1.

for it. In order to identify respondents who oppose this specific compromise, we asked all respondents, after they read the vignette, whether they would have preferred that the senator voted the other way on the bill. We used this to identify who opposed the compromise. For example, a respondent who was assigned to the compromise condition where her senator voted for the compromise proposal was asked "Would you have preferred that your Senator voted against the bill?" Response options were yes and no. If she said she would have preferred that her senator vote against the bill, we coded this as opposition to the compromise. Two-thirds of co-partisan, self-identified primary voters preferred that the legislator support the compromise; a third preferred that the legislator vote against the compromise. This disapproving third may be exactly the primary voters about whom legislators are concerned. The only variable that predicts voters' preferences for whether the senator should vote yes or no on the specific compromise is the extremity of their ideology; those with the most extreme ideologies are less likely to prefer that the senator vote for the compromise. No other political or demographic variable predicts opposition to the specific compromise.[13]

Figure 5.5 shows that these co-partisan primary voters who oppose the specific compromise punish legislators for compromising. The figure illustrates the impact of compromise on approval and vote intention among the third of primary voters in our sample who preferred that the senator kill the bill. For these voters, compromising on the bill has

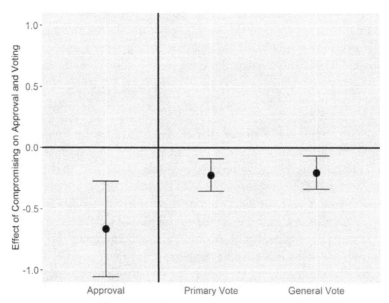

FIGURE 5.5. Voters who oppose the particular compromise have lower approval of and are less likely to vote for senators who compromise.
Note: Effect of compromising is measured as the difference between the average response in the compromise and no compromise conditions. Bars represent 95% confidence intervals. The solid line between the dependent variables highlights that the scale of the first measure (approval) is different from the scale of the next two measures (vote intention). For approval, the dependent variable ranges from 1 (strongly disapprove) to 6 (strongly approve). For primary and general election vote, the dependent variable is a binary measure where voting for the member is a 1.

[13] We tested whether identification as an extreme ideologue, identification as a strong partisan, voting in the primary election, being a contributor of money to candidates/parties, favorability toward Indivisible/Resist, favorability toward the Tea Party, age, race, education, and income were correlated with opposing the specific compromise offered in the vignette.

a significant negative effect on their approval of the senator (−0.66, p = 0.001, two-sided) and a significant negative effect on their intention to vote for the legislator in the primary (−0.22, p = 0.001, two-sided) and general elections (−0.20, p = 0.004, two-sided). This suggests that there is a subset of voters who not only oppose compromise but *will* punish the legislator for compromising.[14] In our study, about one-third of the co-partisan primary voters opposed the compromise. In practice, the number of voters who oppose the compromise may differ by issue, and groups of primary voters who oppose various compromises or the possibility that more than a third will oppose a particular compromise can readily restrain legislators from compromising. The results suggest that a consequential portion of the relevant primary electorate may punish a legislator in the primary and this may worry legislators, especially if the opponent emphasizes a particular compromise that angered those voters.

DISCUSSION

Our survey experiment shows that compromise improves most voters' assessment of senators, but not for those voters who oppose the specific compromise. In the sample as a whole, being told that their senator voted for the compromise proposal increased public approval by almost 0.5 on a scale of 1–6. Even primary voters – whether identified by their own report that they voted in the primary election or by being co-partisans, strong partisans, donors, or those who favor the Tea Party or Indivisible movements – on average approve more of legislators who vote for the compromise. This suggests that legislators' concern about voter punishment is not a concern about all voters (or even all primary voters) but rather a concern about a small segment of voters – the subset who explicitly oppose a given compromise.

Legislators have two good reasons to be more concerned about voter punishment in primary elections than in general elections. First, punishing a legislator by voting for the opposing candidate may be more palatable for co-partisan voters in the primary because they are still

---

[14] We caution that opposition to the specific compromise was evaluated after the treatment and measures of the dependent variables. While post-treatment measures can introduce bias (Montgomery et al. 2018), bias is less of a concern if the variable is capturing how they would have responded to the proposal had they responded prior to receiving the treatment. Here we assume the survey responses are unlikely to be affected by the treatment condition of whether the legislator supported or opposed the compromise.

voting for a candidate from their own party, rather than defecting to the other party in the general election.[15] Second, the co-partisan voters who are willing to punish compromise make up a greater proportion of the primary electorate than the general electorate. So if a compromise vote is likely to hurt a legislator in the general election, it will hurt her even more in the primary. Thus, when legislators think about the potential downside of a compromise vote, it is unsurprising that they focus on the primary election. Our results indicate that they can locate punishment even more specifically in the subset of the primary electorate that opposes specific compromises.

The results reported in this chapter also highlight the importance of voters who care deeply about a given issue, what Converse (1964) called the "issue public." Most voters do not judge politicians by the particular policy stances that they take (Lenz 2013), but this does not mean that it is irrational to fear punishment from those who care deeply about a given issue. Some voters are willing to vote against politicians on the basis of a single vote (Nyhan et al. 2012) and issue accountability for individual members of Congress appears to exist, at least on salient issues (Canes-Wrone et al. 2011). We found that those who oppose the specific compromise – even though it moved the policy outcome closer to their preference – disapprove more of legislators who vote for the compromise and are less likely to vote for the compromising legislator.

Voters who oppose compromise on a specific issue are likely members of an issue public (which need not mean they are single-issue voters). These issue public voters can be consequential for compromise in two ways. First, because members of an issue public generally take more extreme stances on the issue they care about (Krosnick and Telhami 1995; Claassen and Nicholson 2013), seek out more information about that issue (Iyengar et al. 2008), express their opinions through activism, including letter-writing and financial contributions to lobbying organizations (see e.g., Krosnick et al. 1994), and form their vote choices on the basis of those issues (Krosnick 1990), these voters may have outsized influence on legislators' perceptions and electoral fates. In addition to voting against the incumbent, they may donate and mobilize others. If issue public voters are willing to vote

---

[15] Our dependent variable asked whether the respondent would vote for the senator in the general election, with response options of yes or no. It is possible that "no" indicated an intention to stay home on Election Day instead of voting for the challenger from the opposing party, but this would represent a smaller threat than affirmatively voting for a primary challenger.

against an incumbent for a given compromise vote, they – or a group aligned with them – might also be willing to recruit and support a strong primary challenger. A challenger might champion their cause as a path to victory. These actions can be consequential, especially in low turnout primary elections.

The response to the budget compromise in Illinois illustrates how a subset of voters who care deeply about an issue may be instrumental in facilitating punishment of legislators who compromise. Anti-tax issue-related groups played a key role in organizing voter opposition to the compromise, both before and after the vote. Certainly, only a few voters would contact legislators with the kind of extreme language that Illinois legislators reported. But even a small group of angry voters could mobilize broader opposition and help promote a primary challenger so they present a threat that gives incumbent legislators pause.

Because of uncertainty about which compromise votes will lead to consequential voter punishment, legislators have incentives to reject many compromises. Recall the example of former Republican Majority Leader Eric Cantor. When Cantor started to work toward bipartisan compromise on comprehensive immigration reform, there were few reasons to believe that it would hurt him in the primary. After all, the pro-business wing of the Republican Party has traditionally supported immigration as a way to recruit labor for the workforce. Also, reform discussions included more support for border security. Yet David Brat, his primary challenger, successfully painted Cantor's support for reform as evidence of selling out and supporting amnesty. If Cantor had known that this issue would be the centerpiece of Brat's successful campaign, he likely would not have supported reform. The difficulty is that legislators do not always know ex-ante which compromise votes will mobilize primary voters or even challengers against them. As a result, cautious legislators have incentives to reject many compromises, even if these proposals have the support of the majority of their voters.

Second, even if the voters who are willing to punish for a given compromise are small in number, they may be consequential for electoral prospects if there are several groups who all care about their own, different issue. For instance, a small group of voters who oppose compromise on an energy bill, combined with a small group of voters who oppose compromise on a budget bill may, together, amount to a sizable block. If a legislator alienates enough primary voters by supporting compromise proposals it could lead to electoral defeat. We find that those who oppose a given compromise punish their legislator for a compromise vote across the issues of creating new jobs, making the US energy secure, balancing the budget, and securing Social Security and Medicare,[16] suggesting that voter punishment can occur on many kinds of issues. Moreover, legislators often face hundreds of roll call votes in a session. For example, the House of Representatives had 500 recorded votes in 2018. Legislators may well be wary of voting for compromises because they are concerned with the electoral consequences that might arise from an accumulation of compromises that each alienate a different subset of primary voters. Thus, if legislators think that there are enough such voters on a given issue or that the small subsets who are willing to punish them electorally may accumulate across many issues, they may avoid votes for compromise because of a worry that these voters will punish them.

This raises the question of whether there are institutional changes or negotiating strategies that might enable legislators to more freely negotiate and consider compromises. Are there ways to insulate the negotiation process from the small group of voters who deeply oppose compromise? Perhaps there are negotiating strategies that can help lawmakers avoid the ire of groups that oppose compromise and effectively represent the many constituents who approve of legislators who compromise. The next chapter tests two reform strategies for structuring negotiations to increase the likelihood that legislators will vote for compromise proposals.

---

[16] Although the small number of people in the survey who oppose each given compromise means that pooling the issues is necessary for statistical power, point estimates for each separate issue area are negative.

6

Structuring Negotiations in the Shadow
of Primary Voter Punishment

[Compromise] happens more often than you think. Just tends to be on issues which are not 'above the fold.'
2017 NCSL Attendee 105

This book started with the puzzling finding that many legislators are voting against half-loaf compromises that would produce policy changes they support. Legislators reject these half-loaf offers, in part, because they believe that a group of primary voters will punish legislators who support compromises. This fear can prevent legislators from even engaging in serious negotiations because they do not want to appear as though they are willing to capitulate on issues that core voters care about. Yet if they are not willing to seriously engage in these discussions, they are unlikely to reach a compromise deal.

Solutions may lie in creating institutions or norms that allow legislators to insulate the negotiation process from the public. The way negotiations are structured affects the success of those deliberations (Karpowitz and Mendelberg 2007; Karpowitz et al. 2012). When negotiations are not under public scrutiny, legislators may have the freedom to consider concessions that enable them to reach a compromise. As the quote at the beginning of this chapter suggests, many compromises occur on issues outside the public eye and not at the top of the newspaper's front page. This suggests there may be reforms that make compromise less risky.

Our in-person, survey experiments with attendees at the National Conference of State Legislature's (NCSL) 2016 and 2017 annual Legislative Summits evaluated two proposed means for facilitating compromise. In both years, we rented a booth in the exhibit hall and recruited state legislators and their staff to participate in studies of their decision making. In the experiments, legislators and staff were exposed to different negotiation scenarios to see whether changes to the process would alter their ability to reach a compromise. Here, we focus on the results for the legislators in the sample.[1]

The first NCSL experiment assessed whether compromise might be easier to achieve if legislators agree on the broad goals of the policy before negotiating over the details to achieve those goals (Huntsman and Manchin 2014). The group No Labels has proposed this method of negotiation to overcome gridlock in Congress. They argue, for example, that if Republicans and Democrats could first agree that they should lower the debt by a particular amount then it would be easier for them to find a compromise on the mix of tax increases and spending cuts used to achieve that goal. The 2016 NCSL experiment provides no evidence for this claim, which is consistent with the fear of voter punishment being a major driver of legislators' rejection of compromise solutions. Simply agreeing on the goals does nothing to limit the threat of voter punishment in primaries because primary voters care about the means used to achieve a policy outcome and not just the outcome itself.

The second NCSL experiment tests whether negotiating in private rather than in public improves the chances of achieving compromise. While sunshine laws, which increase government transparency by requiring that legislators conduct more of their business in public, are introduced to improve representation and accountability, they also give legislators less room to maneuver. Because at least some voters punish compromise, legislators may be less likely to agree to compromise solutions when they know that those voters are closely following the negotiation. Bargaining in private may shield them from revealing the detailed back-and-forth of the bargaining and thus avoid triggering punishment from voters. In short, public scrutiny of negotiations may increase accountability to some voters at the expense of consideration of compromise solutions (Warren et al. 2016).

The experiment shows that legislators randomly assigned to negotiating in private rather than in public report they are more likely to achieve a compromise solution. However, negotiating in private is not without

---

[1] The first question on the survey asked for the respondent's position (legislator or staff), which was also clearly indicated on their badges. Analyses here restrict the sample to only legislators. The results are very similar when the full sample of respondents is used.

issues: legislators say they are less willing to attend a private negotiation. Private meetings make it difficult for legislators to claim credit for working on issues relevant to voters. And they may face negative consequences from the secrecy of private meetings. Legislators work hard to gain voters' trust (Fenno 1978) and may worry that private negotiations will jeopardize that trust. Thus, as legislators decide how to structure negotiations, they must weigh the benefits of private negotiations in facilitating compromise against the drawbacks of private negotiations for other aspects of their representative role.

NO LABELS AND A FOCUS ON SHARED GOALS

At the 2016 NCSL Legislative Summit, we tested the argument that the path to successful compromise is to first have both sides agree on the end goal, an approach that the group No Labels has advocated. No Labels formed in 2010 in response to the gridlock in Washington, DC, with the motto to "stop fighting, start fixing" and has been working to get legislators to move forward on common ground proposals. In the words of their website, this bipartisan group of politicians seeks to be a "stabilizing force within our Congress; a bloc of elected officials who combine ideological independence and common sense with a willingness to reach across the aisle to get things done" (No Labels 2017). No Labels has advocated for several bills that have made it through Congress and helped create the Problem Solver Caucus, a group of bipartisan legislators who work together to find areas of consensus. As of 2018, this group had forty-eight members – half Democrats and half Republicans.

One of No Label's main arguments is that leaders are more likely to solve problems if they first unite behind shared goals and then determine the process or details needed to achieve those goals. No Labels argues that if people have a shared end goal and focus on that goal, it leads them to consider proposals and compromises that they would not have considered otherwise. Eighty members of Congress supported the No Labels National Strategic Agenda, highlighting four goals for policy change with majority public support in 2014. The logic behind this strategy was detailed in the founders' book, *No Labels: A Shared Vision for a Stronger America* (Huntsman and Manchin 2014), that features examples of and suggestions for successfully achieving compromise. For instance, the 2010 Simpson-Bowles commission was tasked with reducing the federal debt to below 60% of the GDP, which would require a combination of strategies. That shared goal became the framework for discussion and allowed some proposals (e.g., tax increases that Republicans did not want or spending cuts that Democrats wished to avoid) to be considered that would not have been on the table for partisan legislators if the negotiators had started with the proposal and not the shared goal (Huntsman and Manchin 2014). In the *No Labels* book, Mark McLarty, White House Chief of Staff under President Bill Clinton, points to multiple examples where legislation was successful and had bipartisan support because of the focus on shared goals – NAFTA, the 1996 Personal Responsibility and Work Opportunity Act (known as welfare-to-work), and the 1997 budget agreement (Huntsman and Manchin 2014, location 1123). Similarly Harvard Business School professor Michael Porter describes a strategy for using shared goals as a framework for subsequent legislation (Huntsman and Manchin 2014, position 704). In all cases, No Labels proponents argue that it is easier to build a bipartisan coalition and reach compromises when the legislators share a commitment to the end goal.

In addition, there are a broad set of social-psychological reasons that support the argument that agreement on principles can help to facilitate compromise. First, a focus on shared goals could help move negotiation into a more integrative and deliberative form that emphasizes what each side gains, or at least where there is mutual creation of value (Warren et al. 2016, 154). Second, developing a shared identity can overcome bias and prejudice (Gaertner and Dovidio 2011) and leads to a preference for greater equality (Kramer et al. 1993), both of which should facilitate compromise. Third, these end goals likely reflect the underlying values of the legislators (Schwartz 1977, 1992). People who are asked to affirm their values are more open to supporting opposition party candidates (Binning et al. 2010) and more willing to make concessions (Cohen et al. 2007). These findings align with No Labels' argument that the very act of agreeing on broad goals and reaffirming values may make compromise easier for elected officials.

No Labels has identified several areas where their approach is most likely to work. These are policy areas where there is likely to be consensus on the end goal and where a combination of approaches may be necessary to achieve that goal. Most prominently, they identified four policy goals in their National Strategic Agenda that could plausibly receive strong, bipartisan support:

- Creating 25 million jobs over the next 10 years
- Securing Social Security and Medicare for the next 75 years

- Balancing the federal budget by 2030
- Making America energy secure by 2024.

Each of these goals garners majority support from the public, including support from both Republicans and Democrats (No Labels 2016). What differs between parties in each case is the preferred means to achieve the goal. For example, their respective platforms in 2016 show that both Republicans and Democrats support energy security but differ on the means by which they would increase domestic energy production. Republicans want to achieve this goal through "development of all forms of energy that are marketable in a free economy without subsidies, including coal, oil, natural gas, nuclear power, and hydropower," whereas Democrats would prefer to achieve it by "building a clean energy economy" (Democratic Platform Committee 2016; Republican Platform Committee 2016).

Heavy hitters in the broader policy community also advocate for shared principles as a way to achieve compromise. For instance, policy advocates such as the AARP argue that Congress should focus on the larger goals of economic growth, jobs, health, and financial security and then find policies to meet those goals (Rand 2013). While not as explicit as No Labels' argument, such commentary suggests that political actors believe that compromise would be easier to achieve if legislators focused on the end goal first and then debated the means to achieve it. In fact, moving from an initial focus on shared end goals to a strategic plan to address those goals is a common route for businesses, as well as for governments in countries like China (Chen 1993), where strategic plans are common (Zartman and Berman 1982; Pendergast 1990).

However, legislators' fear of voter retribution is a reason to be skeptical that agreement on principles and end goals will increase the likelihood of compromise. Many legislators believe primary voters, or at least an important subset of primary voters, oppose compromise. While our results in Chapter 5 suggest that most voters do not punish compromise, about a third of primary voters in our study oppose it. Further, these co-partisan, primary voters who oppose compromise are willing to punish co-partisan incumbents who compromise. These voters appear to view compromise as an abandonment of principles and a form of political treachery. These same voters are also likely concerned about the means used to achieve policy ends and may care deeply whether an issue like energy security is resolved through expanded production of fossil fuels or expanded production of green energy. In keeping with Egan (2014), we found that the politically sophisticated voters who are likely to make up the primary electorate are more likely to prefer inaction over using a means they do not like to achieve the policy goal.

Voters Care about the Means Used to Achieve a Policy

Our survey results confirm that primary voters care about the means used to achieve goals. In the December 2017 survey (see Chapter 5 for full details), voters were asked about how they would prefer to accomplish four goals. Those goals were creating new jobs, balancing the budget, securing America's energy independence, and securing Social Security and Medicare – all of which align with No Label's strategic agenda. For each goal, voters had three options for how to achieve the goal: a conservative means, a liberal means, and using a combination of both means. Here, for example, is the wording of the question regarding balancing the budget (the wording for the other questions is provided in Chapter 5):

Which of the following best describes your attitude on balancing the budget:

- The government should balance the budget by cutting spending on social programs
- The government should balance the budget by increasing taxes
- The government should balance the budget by increasing taxes and cutting spending

Later in the study the respondent was asked the following question about one of the issues where they had taken a party-consistent position:

You stated that you would like to {achieve the policy goal} by {means they had chosen}. Would you still want to {achieve the policy goal} if you could only do it entirely through {the means they had not chosen}?

For example, a voter who chose the liberal position for how to balance the budget would have seen: "You stated that you would like to balance the budget by increasing taxes. Would you still want to balance the budget if you could only do it entirely through cutting spending on social programs?" Only 29% of self-identified primary voters and only 32% of all respondents say that they would want to achieve the goal if it were done by their non-preferred means. The majority of voters care about the means used to achieve the agreed-upon goal.

Moreover, about a third of the public view compromise in politics as selling out one's principles (Hutchings et al. 2017). Getting legislators to agree on the end goal may not resolve the threat that they face from voters if they choose to compromise on the means.

With these competing considerations in mind – No Labels and social-psychological arguments in favor of emphasizing end goals as a route to compromise and our findings about perceptions of voter punishment in primaries as a limiting factor to this approach – the 2016 study tested whether an initial focus on shared goals increases legislators' willingness to support compromise on the means for reaching that goal.

Testing Agreement on Shared Goals and Compromise

To test the No Labels' argument, a survey experiment on a sample of state legislators attending the 2016 NCSL Legislative Summit randomized the focus on shared goals versus jumping to consideration of one's favored policy alternative and tests whether this affects the likelihood of reaching a compromise. In an ideal world, we might work with several committees or policy commissions tasked with addressing important policy issues, randomizing one to focus first on shared goals and the other to begin by introducing policy proposals to address the issue, but such large-scale research designs are not feasible. Therefore, we presented a vignette-style experiment to 65 legislators and 93 staff. The results below are based on the responses from state legislators.

In the experimental portion of the study, respondents were told that they would enter a negotiation with someone referred to as Legislator Smith on national issues that affect the states and their citizens. Legislator Smith was fictional and his party and position were manipulated within the experiment. Participants were first asked about the goals they would like to achieve from the list identified by No Labels. This strategy creates a most-likely case for finding an effect; if agreement on broad goals does not yield more compromise in the cases where agreement is easier, it is even less likely that this strategy will lead to compromise on issues where there is little bipartisan agreement on the end goal. Respondents indicated which of the No Labels goals they agreed with: (1) We should create new jobs, (2) We should make the US energy secure, (3) We should balance the federal budget, and (4) We should secure Social Security and

Medicare.[2] Legislators were then randomly assigned to negotiate on one of the issues they had listed as a priority.

The study then diverged between participants in the control and shared goals treatment conditions. In the control condition, legislators were told that they would negotiate with Legislator Smith about the assigned issue. We then immediately presented them with two alternative means for addressing that issue and asked which they would prefer. For instance, if legislators were assigned to negotiate over job creation, the competing means of addressing the issue were tax incentives for companies who make new hires and expanding government activities that stimulate the economy. By contrast, legislators in the shared goals treatment condition were told they would negotiate with Legislator Smith about the assigned issue and then asked to use paper and pencil to give one reason why this issue is a top priority for them. This was included as part of the treatment because writing about a goal can be a form of mental stimulation that allows the legislator to envision the goal better (Taylor et al. 1998; Taylor and Pham 1999). Further, research in psychology suggests that justifying one's stance to others affects the complexity of information processing (Tetlock 1983; Lerner and Tetlock 1999) and that more consideration of an issue leads to more thoughtful, conscious processing (Petty and Cacioppo 1984, 1986). In survey research, scholars often ask respondents to write down why they hold a policy view or a party identification to induce them to be more committed to that view or identity (Bolsen et al. 2014). So writing about the goal should further cement the legislator's commitment to the end goal.

Legislators appeared to take the writing task seriously. The average time spent on this task was 55 seconds, and the median time was 42 seconds. What they wrote on the paper also shows evidence of compliance with the treatment and thoughtful consideration of the issue. Moreover, the comments were focused on the end goal itself, not on the means they would use to reach it. Comments included the following:

- "Interested in prioritizing Social Security and Medicare because it is up to the government to responsibly use the money paid into a program for that program."

---

[2] If participants selected a fifth option "none of the above," they were asked "Of these four issues, which is the most important to you? That is, if you had to choose to pursue one of these goals, which would you choose?" If participants selected "I would never pursue any of these goals," they would have been dropped from the study. All of the state legislators in the sample chose at least one of the four goals.

- "Less reliance on outside energy will inherently benefit the U.S. – create jobs and less fluctuation on global output and control."
- "Creating jobs in our state is very important to our future: both economic viability and opportunities for growth and to generate revenues to replace industry we are losing."
- "Jobs = improved middle class = stable society = more taxes = greater country and possibilities."
- "It's important to ensure our citizens are able to receive health care and able to take care of themselves in their old age, regardless of whether they earned/saved enough over the years. Everyone should have access to life's basic necessities."
- "A good job eliminates many other problems from federal spending to reducing crime."
- "We can't keep foisting debt on our children."

When the legislators in the shared goals condition finished writing about the goal, they placed the paper in a cup on the table and continued with the study. They were then told that Legislator Smith shares this goal as a top priority and they were provided with a statement from him. For instance, on the topic of securing Social Security and Medicare, the legislators were told:

Like you, Legislator Smith told us that securing Social Security and Medicare was a top issue priority. He wrote: "It is crucial for us to secure Social Security and Medicare. When these critical programs are safe, the government and the people are in a better position to thrive. Rather than having to worry about long-term economic security of these programs, we are able to focus on growth and new opportunities. This is a top priority for me."

The statement from Legislator Smith demonstrated to participants that they would be negotiating with a legislator who shared their goal.

After writing down their own reason for viewing this goal as a priority and seeing Legislator Smith's shared commitment to this goal, the legislators were asked which of two alternative tools they would favor for addressing this issue. In the case of securing Social Security and Medicare, the respondent chose between decreased benefits to recipients or increased taxes to cover costs. The question wording and alternatives were the same as those used in the control condition.

All participants then received the same negotiation vignette. The vignette said that Legislator Smith would prefer to address this issue through the opposite means of what the respondent had chosen. In all cases, Legislator Smith was assigned to the party that would be congruent with the means that he preferred.[3] For example, if a respondent wanted to cover the costs of securing Social Security by increasing taxes, Legislator Smith was said to support decreased benefits to recipients of Social Security and to be a Republican. All participants were then asked whether they would be willing to publicly support and vote for a compromise proposal if Legislator Smith would also support it. In the compromise proposal the legislator's preferred policy tool covered half of the gap and Legislator Smith's preferred policy tool covered the other half.

Overall, 52% of the legislator participants say that they would support the compromise proposal. Support for compromise was marginally higher in the pooled legislator and staff sample (58% supported compromise). While this compromise is like the compromise offered to legislators on the gas tax in Chapter 2 in that it is an offer to meet in the middle, it may be more difficult for legislators to accept because of the party label of the opposing legislator and because the compromise also includes the use of the means preferred by Legislator Smith.

Agreeing first on broad goals has no effect on compromise. Figure 6.1 shows the percentage of each group of legislators that accept the compromise proposal. In the control group – where legislators moved immediately to focusing on policy means – 51% of legislators accept the compromise. In the treatment group – where legislators first focused on the end goal – 54% of legislators accept the compromise, an insignificant increase in their willingness to compromise ($p = 0.86$, two-sided). In short, there is no evidence that the No Labels' approach of focusing on shared goals increases the willingness to support a compromise that meets in the middle, with half of the goal being achieved through the legislator's preferred alternative and half through the less preferred alternative.

Table 6.1 uses OLS regression models to show that the null effect of the No Labels approach is robust to various model specifications and ways of subsetting the sample. Column 1 shows the results for all legislators (as in the figure above). Column 2 adds control variables for the

---

[3] The sample skewed Democratic: 64% of the legislators identified as Democrats and 36% identified as Republicans. Unsurprisingly, then, the majority, 56%, of the legislators took the more liberal position. Partisan legislators overwhelmingly favored the alternative that we would associate with their party. 83% of Democratic and Republican legislators selected the party-consistent alternative. This meant that assigning Legislator Smith to the other policy tool also usually assigned him to the opposite party from the respondent. We present robustness checks that limit the sample to those who chose party-consistent means in Table 6.1.

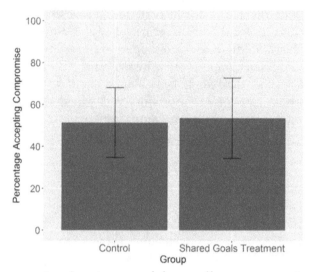

FIGURE 6.1. Agreeing on goals has no effect on compromise.
Note: Bars represent 95% confidence intervals.

TABLE 6.1. *The shared goals approach is ineffective at increasing compromise*

Dependent Variable = Accept Compromise	(1) Legislators	(2) Legislators	(3) Legislators with Party Consistent Position	(4) Legislators and Staff
Shared Goals Treatment	0.022 (0.13)	−0.0083 (0.14)	−0.17 (0.14)	−0.0011 (0.079)
Republican	—	−0.13 (0.14)	—	—
Issue = jobs	—	−0.0046 (0.19)	—	—
Issue = energy	—	−0.31 (0.25)	—	—
Issue = SS and Medicare	—	−0.4 (0.2)	—	—
Intercept	0.51* (0.083)	0.71* (0.16)	0.48* (0.087)	0.58* (0.054)
N	65	65	52	158
R-Squared	0.00048	0.14	0.027	1.3×10^{-6}

Note: Dependent variable is 1 if accepted compromise, 0 if not. Models estimated using OLS regression. Standard errors in parentheses.

* $p < 0.05$ (two-sided).

party of the legislator and the issue area they selected as important and were assigned to. Column 3 includes only the legislators who took a party-consistent position on the means for achieving the goal. Column 4 includes both legislators and their staff. The shared goals treatment does not significantly increase compromise in any specification or subgroup of respondents, and the point estimate is negative in three of the four models. It is clear that the initial focus on shared goals does not increase legislators' willingness to compromise.

Although having legislators agree on shared goals does not increase the likelihood of compromise, it is important to recognize the scope conditions of this result. We looked at a single instance of negotiation with an individual with whom the legislator did not have any other familiarity. While this achieves the aim of testing the core logic of No Labels' argument, it does not embed the treatment in other activities that may facilitate compromise or even interact with the focus on shared goals. The Problem Solver Caucus, for example, might facilitate face-to-face, repeated interactions that would better facilitate compromise.

Nonetheless, the design maintains many features that would suggest relatively high external validity. These are salient public issues on which legislators are likely to have thought about their issue position, and the negotiation proposed the type of compromise that may be expected when negotiation occurs between two parties. For instance, this style of negotiation, where the proposal includes part of what each side wants, is common in state and federal compromises. In 2017, Colorado Democrats opposed legislation to save rural hospitals from massive cuts when it included both their favored alternatives (fee reclassification and increased funding for schools) and Republican's favored alternative (an increase in the cost of prescription refills) (Perkins 2017). Likewise, the compromise in the vignette resembles the budget sequestration/debt ceiling compromise brokered by Senator Murkowski (R-AK) and colleagues where each side achieved some of want they wanted (see Chapter 4).

The choice of issues in the research design was also a best-case scenario for the No Labels treatment to have an effect because agreement on broad goals is particularly likely to exist on these issues. Moreover, elections were not salient in our design, which may have meant legislators were less focused on the electoral consequences of a compromise or the desire to differentiate their party from the opposing party.

Given that the study design captured the core logic of No Labels' argument, had high external validity, and was a best-case scenario for finding an effect, the null findings are compelling evidence that simply focusing on shared goals before negotiating over means does not improve legislators' willingness to compromise. It remains possible that spending time with legislators from the opposing party and building mutual respect may help legislators reach compromise. However, the core element of focusing on shared goals shows little evidence of changing legislator's willingness to compromise. Given legislators' concern about voter retribution in primaries for compromising, this makes sense. A compromise may look just as bad to primary voters, regardless of whether the legislator got there by focusing on shared end goals. Simply agreeing on broad goals does not necessarily alter legislators' calculus of whether they will be punished by primary voters for compromising because accepting the compromise may appear to be an abandonment of principles.

PRIVATE NEGOTIATIONS AND COMPROMISE

If the perception of electoral retribution is a crucial obstacle to compromise, insulating members from the threat of retribution may increase the likelihood of reaching a compromise agreement. Negotiating in private may be one way to insulate legislators from constituents who oppose compromise. Private negotiation could be effective by allowing legislators to agree on a deal without pressure from constituents and the need to posture before them.

Working in private, legislators can form coalitions of support on what may otherwise be conflictual issues (Curry 2015). An important part of reaching a deal is first learning what disagreements exist and what everyone is willing to give up (Karpowitz and Mansbridge 2005). But this rarely happens in public. As one of the attendees at the 2017 NCSL meeting put it, compromise can be hard when legislators "stick to what voters understand (talking points) and not more complicated compromises" (2017 NCSL Attendee 248).

If legislators negotiate in public, they have incentives to be hesitant to relay what they will give up because they do not want their voters to know this without also showing the voters what concessions they extracted in return. Constituents often know little about what is and is not feasible in a legislature (Gilmour 1995, 25–37; Binder and Lee 2016, 95–96) and may be quick to negatively judge a legislator who readily negotiates and considers partial solutions. Formal models show that when legislators bargain publicly they are less likely to budge because they do not want voters to see them as capitulating and may even want to make the opposition look bad (Groseclose and McCarty 2001). Thus privacy can be vital to making compromise possible.

Deliberations over the federal budget in 2011, for example, failed when the negotiation became public. President Barack Obama and House Speaker John Boehner were both interested in finding a way to rewrite the tax code, reduce the cost of entitlements, and cut the deficit, and they set out to come to a "grand bargain" on these issues. Each had a preferred means for achieving their shared goals, and they attempted to reach a compromise by negotiating in private. But the deal fell apart after the elements of the potential deal leaked to other members of Congress and to the public (Binder and Lee 2016, 107). Both sides blamed the other for being unable to deliver on what they promised due to the recalcitrance of their caucus. At the same time both had reasons to avoid revealing what they were willing to concede in the negotiation. Matt Bai's commentary in the *New York Times* emphasized that compromise had become impossible specifically because of the sunlight shone on the matter:

There is a practical reason for this. Both sides knew that if the most crucial and contested details of their deliberations became public, it would complicate relationships with some of their most important constituencies in Washington – or worse ... Obama and Boehner have clung to their separate realities not just because it's useful to blame each other for the political dysfunction in Washington, but because neither wants to talk about just how far he was willing to go. (Bai 2012)

Social psychology research on negotiation generally shows that private negotiations can make individuals more flexible by limiting the influence of audiences (Walton and McKersie 1965; Druckman 1994) and by reducing pressures to save face (Brown 1977). Experimental research shows that whether the negotiation is held at a peripheral (private) or central (public) location and whether there is limited (private) or wide (public) media coverage of the negotiation affect people's flexibility in negotiation as well as their actual ability to reach a compromise (Druckman 1993, 1995; Druckman and Druckman 1996). And indeed, there are many examples of successful negotiations carried out in private. For example, the Trans-Pacific Partnership (TPP) was a large trade deal finalized in 2015 and negotiated largely outside the public eye (Bradner 2015).[4] The majority of Republicans in both houses, joined by 13 Democratic senators and 28 Democratic members of the House, gave President Obama trade-promotion authority to negotiate a deal that

---

[4] President Donald Trump took the US out of the trade partnership once he was in office.

would subsequently be considered by Congress with no amendments. This allowed the details of the trade deal to be negotiated without the public attention accorded to Congressional negotiations and floor voting on amendments. While many criticized the private nature of the resulting negotiations (e.g., Zornick 2014), President Obama defended the privacy of the negotiations as necessary due to the large number of actors involved. As he said at a town hall at the time, "If you are negotiating with 12 countries and there's no space for everyone to agree on the deal … then it would never get done … The nature of the trade agreement is so many interests are involved, so what we've done instead is close the initial deal" (Spetalnick 2015).

It was not the first time an official cited privacy as nurturing compromise. Representative Henry Waxman (D-CA) (2009, 137), reflecting on his successful pesticide negotiation with Representative Thomas Bliley (R-VA) in the 1990s, highlighted the privacy of the negotiations: "We implicitly trusted one another not to go public, had things not worked out, with the details of what the other side had been willing to concede." The revised regulations they agreed on set a single standard for pesticide chemical residue allowed on Americans' food, both fresh and processed. This agreement expanded the percentage of foods covered and consolidated a previously fragmented system of pesticide tolerances. It passed the House with bipartisan unanimity, despite facing opposition from some environmental interest groups that thought it did not go far enough to protect consumers and regulate industry (Bornemeier 1996). Similarly, Senators Trent Lott (R-MS) and Tom Daschle (D-SD) credit bipartisan agreement on the 2001 No Child Left Behind Act to private meetings in offices and conference rooms off of the House and Senate floors (2017, 94). These examples, in conjunction with the social psychology research on negotiation, suggest that negotiating in private may facilitate reaching a compromise.

Testing the Impact of Private Negotiations on Compromise

We designed an experiment to test the impact of private negotiations on legislators' support for compromise. We carried out the test by renting a booth at the 2017 NCSL Summit in Boston. During the three days of the conference we invited legislators and their staff to participate in our study; 205 legislators and 141 staff members participated.[5] The results presented here focus on only the state legislators.

---

[5] Among state legislators who participated in this experiment, 34% were Republicans and 66% were Democrats.

The survey asked respondents to think about their own state and to pick one area they think should get a greater share of the budget and one that should get a smaller share than it does now.[6] The options came from a list of common budget items given in *The Fiscal Survey of the States*.[7] The choices were transportation, health, K-12 education, higher education, public assistance, and law enforcement. We randomly chose one of the areas they indicated and asked respondents to consider the situation given in Figure 6.2, which randomized whether the negotiation would be held in public or private. The parts of the vignette in {curly brackets}

Imagine that about half of the legislators agree with you (i.e., they want to {increase / decrease} spending on {chosen area} like you do), while the other half want to keep last year's spending level.

As the details of the bill dealing with the spending are being finalized, the key {Republican legislators / Democratic legislators} on the other side of the issue (those for keeping last year's level of spending), ask to discuss the issue **[during a public meeting / in a closed-door meeting]** in order to work out a compromise. The press has been paying close attention to {chosen area} spending [and the local paper is expected to attend and report on the meeting. The press is interested in reporting on the details of negotiations, including the back and forth of proposals and counterproposals. / but no press will be allowed at the meeting. However, the local paper is interested in reporting on the final outcome of the negotiation.]

How likely would you be to agree to discuss the issue [in a public meeting / in a closed door meeting]?
  Extremely likely
  Somewhat likely
  Neither likely nor unlikely
  Somewhat unlikely
  Extremely unlikely

If you did agree to meet, how likely would you be to reach a compromise during that [public / private] meeting that both sides would support?
  Extremely likely
  Somewhat likely
  Neither likely nor unlikely
  Somewhat unlikely
  Extremely unlikely

FIGURE 6.2. Text of vignette for private versus public negotiations.
Note: Elements in square brackets were randomized. Elements in curly brackets were automatically programmed into the vignette based upon the respondent's earlier answers.

[6] Reflecting partisan preferences for generally smaller or larger government, some legislators would only choose either an area to increase or to decrease spending but not both. In such cases, we asked them about the area they chose in the rest of the survey.
[7] https://higherlogicdownload.s3.amazonaws.com/NASBO/9d2d2db1-c943-4f1b-b750-ofca152d64c2/UploadedImages/Fiscal%20Survey/Fall%202016%20Fiscal%20Survey%20of%20States%20-%20S.pdf.

were not randomized; they were automatically programmed into the vignette based on the respondent's earlier answers. For example, those who wanted to increase spending on K-12 education were asked about a "situation pertaining to the increase in K-12 education spending...." Similarly, those who self-identified as Democrats were told about "the key Republican legislators" and vice versa for self-identified Republicans.

As Figure 6.2 shows, the legislators were randomly assigned to being asked about bargaining in a public meeting or in a private meeting. We highlighted the nature of the meeting through both the description of the meeting – public or closed-door – and through the extent of the press coverage. If they were assigned to the public negotiation, participants were told that the local paper was expected to attend and report on the meeting, including the back and forth of proposals and counterproposals. This language highlighted that information about what alternatives the legislator proposed or considered would be visible to constituents in the public negotiation. By contrast, if they were assigned to the private negotiation, participants were told that the other side asked to discuss the issue in a closed-door meeting to work out a compromise. They were informed that no press would be allowed at the meeting. Instead, they were told that the local paper was interested in reporting on the final outcome of the negotiation. This language signaled that the back-and-forth of the negotiation and concessions would be private and that only the final agreement would be public. Mentioning the interest of the local paper in both conditions, however, makes the salience of the legislation similar across conditions.

Participants in both the public and private treatments were then asked how likely they would be to meet to discuss this issue in the (public or private) meeting, and, if they did meet, how likely they would be to reach a compromise that both sides would support during that meeting. Figure 6.3 shows the average likelihood of agreeing to meet and of coming to a compromise in the public and private negotiations. The dependent variables range from 1 (=Extremely unlikely) to 5 (=Extremely likely) for agreeing to meet and for likelihood of achieving compromise. Legislators are less likely to agree to discuss the issue when they are assigned to bargain in a private meeting. The average legislator assigned to public negotiation was somewhat likely to meet, but the average legislator assigned to private negotiations was somewhere in between being indifferent about meeting and being somewhat likely to meet. The difference between the public and private negotiations is −0.48 ($p = 0.004$, two-sided). At the same time, legislators believe that they will be more

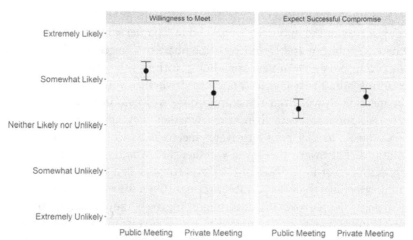

FIGURE 6.3. Legislators say they are less likely to go to a private meeting, but more likely to reach a compromise in a private meeting.
Note: Figure presents the mean response for each condition on each dependent variable along with 95% confidence intervals.

likely to reach a successful compromise agreement if they do negotiate in private. The legislators assigned to the private negotiation are 0.27 points more likely to believe that a compromise would be reached ($p = 0.05$, two-sided).[8] In sum, private negotiations decrease legislators' willingness to meet but increase legislators' confidence that they would reach a compromise.

These results are consistent with the electoral incentives shaping legislators' expectations about bargaining. On the one hand, private meetings may be less attractive to legislators who do not want to alienate voters by appearing to be secretive (Warren et al. 2016, 178). Legislators may worry that negotiating in private meetings may jeopardize the trust they work to build with their voters. By contrast, public meetings provide legislators with a platform to show constituents that they are advocating on their behalf. This is especially true when the issue is salient and high profile. Legislators may thus find public meetings more attractive because it is an opportunity to advertise, claim credit, and win votes.

---

[8] When we consider the responses for both legislators and staffers, there is a negative but non-significant effect of the private treatment (relative to the public treatment) on willingness to meet (difference = –0.19, $p = 0.16$, two-sided) and a positive and significant effect of the private treatment on reaching a compromise (difference = 0.33, $p = 0.002$, two-sided).

Not surprisingly, voters favor public meetings as well. The December 2017 survey of the public we described in Chapter 5 included a vignette where Republican and Democratic members of Congress had reached a compromise on government spending priorities in an upcoming appropriations bill. The vignette randomized whether voters were told that the meeting to work out the compromise was held in public or in private. Respondents were then asked whether they approve of members of Congress having public (private) meetings to work on compromise solutions. They were also asked whether they would have preferred that legislators meet in private (public). Approval is significantly higher for public meetings than for private meetings. On a four-point scale from 1 (=Strongly Disapprove) to 4 (=Strongly Approve), the average approval is 3.2 for public meetings, compared to 2.3 for private meetings ($p < 0.001$, two-sided). Overall, 79% of respondents preferred that legislators meet to work out compromises in public meetings. These findings suggest that legislators are right to be hesitant to meet in private because it may frustrate voters or violate their trust.

On the other hand, private meetings can insulate legislators from the voters who would punish them for compromising. Private meetings allow legislators to share potential concessions with other legislators without having to share them with constituents. Legislators can avoid showing their hands and angering voters without the benefit of achieving a compromise that provides a policy victory. This insulation from voters can be especially valuable for legislators with a substantial number of primary voters who punish compromise. In private meetings, legislators can avoid the grandstanding and talking points necessary to show constituents that they will not cave in to the other side (Patty 2016) and can instead focus on achieving compromise.

Reformers interested in increasing the likelihood that legislators identify and pass compromise deals need to find a way to insulate them from the perceived threat from primary voters. Our results show that negotiating in private may be an effective way of shielding legislators from this perceived electoral threat. Private negotiations lead legislators to believe that there is a greater likelihood that they will achieve a compromise. This does not mean that governing should be done in private; such a remedy would be worse than the problem of gridlock. Voters should learn about the policies that governments pass and they should hold legislators accountable when they do not like the policies that are passed. However, the evidence in this chapter indicates that legislators can and should be given some privacy during the negotiation process so they can consider effective compromise solutions.

DISCUSSION

Many legislators fear retribution from their primary voters if they compromise. When legislators enter a negotiation from this perspective, it can be hard to reach even mutually beneficial compromises, which leads to inaction and gridlock. This chapter suggests that reforms that change the institutional environment surrounding negotiation could solve this problem.

We experimentally tested two solutions for achieving compromise – a focus on shared end goals and negotiating in private rather than public. While the findings provided little support for the idea that getting legislators to focus on shared end goals would improve their willingness to compromise over the means of reaching that goal, we are optimistic that negotiating in private can be part of the solution. Future research can examine additional institutional reforms that could enhance the prospects for reaching compromise. Studying how to structure the privacy of negotiations is a fruitful place to start.

Negotiating in private is a solution that has a long history in American politics and is often used to facilitate deliberation. In fact, the founding documents of this country reflected compromises achieved in closed-door meetings. The Federal Convention to design a U.S. Constitution was closed and secret; the delegates even kept the shades in the room drawn. As one delegate, George Mason, put it to his son:

It is expected our doors will be shut, and communications upon the business of the Convention be forbidden during its sitting. This I think myself a proper precaution to prevent mistakes and misrepresentation until the business shall have been completed, when the whole may have a very different complexion from that in which the several crude indigested parts might in their first shape appear if submitted to the public eye. (Mason 1892, 28)

James Madison later remarked that he did not think the delegates could have come to an agreement on the Constitution if the proceedings had been public (Warren et al. 2016, 175).

More recently, private negotiations have facilitated several bipartisan accomplishments. For example, despite skepticism that the five Democrats and five Republicans on the 9/11 Commission would be able reach a compromise, the group reached consensus on all of its findings and recommendations, including the establishment of a national intelligence director. Professor of international relations at American University Jordan Tamu wrote in the *New York Times* that their success was due to the private nature of the negotiation (Tamu 2011). Similarly, in 2015, Speaker Boehner's and Minority Leader Pelosi's staffs worked out a more permanent fix to Medicare's Sustainable Growth Rate by working in private with key stakeholders behind the scenes (Curry and Lee 2016).[9]

The 1999 Senate impeachment trial of President Clinton further illustrates how the content of deliberation and negotiation changes when discussions are public or private. Republican Senate Majority Leader Trent Lott and Democratic Minority Leader Tom Daschle were initially torn on whether to allow cameras in the impeachment trial. They ended up settling on a compromise – televise the proceedings during the day but no cameras would be allowed after 6 p.m. They noted that it was an "eye-opening experiment" and that the "contrast in the quality of the discussion and the candor from the members was astounding. Senators came up to the podium and poured their hearts out; we all said things that we would never say in front of the cameras" (Lott and Daschle 2017, 53).

In our own study, legislators were significantly more likely to believe they could reach an agreement that both sides would support when they were negotiating in private rather than public. This finding aligns with literature that highlights the downsides of transparency laws that force negotiations into the public eye. Transparency, often stemming from sunshine laws, can have the unintended consequences of making compromise harder to achieve, both by increasing incentives to adhere to party messages and by decreasing attention given to all possible solutions (Binder and Lee 2016, 105–106).

Private negotiations are not without their downsides and members are cognizant of the tradeoffs. "It's difficult to explain to those who elected you that you don't want them to see what you're up to" (Lott and Daschle 2017, 94). Private negotiations raise concerns of a lack of accountability to voters, and may hamper legislators' efforts at credit claiming. The state legislators we surveyed indicated they were less willing to meet to discuss the issue in a private meeting, even though they recognized they would be more likely to reach a compromise in that private meeting. Effectively communicating with voters about the advantages of private negotiations may help reduce the political downsides of meeting in private in the first place. This suggests that future research should consider how to improve public acceptance of private meetings, and whether it is sufficient to ensure that final outcomes are made public

---

[9] The bill ended up passing with a bipartisan supermajority (392-37 in the House, 92-8 in the Senate).

or if the public needs other assurances before they are comfortable letting elected officials hash out compromises behind closed-doors.

With both the pros and cons of private meetings in mind, perhaps one solution is to insulate the process (through private negotiations) *and* better communicate the final compromise to voters. This can allow decision makers to negotiate over their preferred policies rather than focusing on signaling to their constituents (Stasavage 2007). One route to achieving this balance may be to make private meetings more aligned with democratic accountability. Warren et al. (2016, 181–85) provide several suggestions for how closed-door meetings can be more democratically accessible. First, they suggest that citizens should have the opportunity to agree to the decision to negotiate in private. Admittedly, this may be difficult to achieve, except on national security policies or others where the public recognizes the value of secrecy. Second, they suggest that closed-door negotiations are less problematic when constituents have good reasons to trust legislators to act on their behalf; what they term "warranted trust." In the open-ended responses, our legislators echoed this idea, suggesting that it is important to explain their positions to constituents, in part because it can help them gain their constituents' trust. One legislator, when asked how to avoid voter punishment for compromising, emphasized that legislators should "build trust with your constituents... and be able and willing to explain yourself when you disagree" (2017 NCSL Attendee 210). Third, Warren, Mansbridge and co-authors suggest that having all relevant interests represented in the negotiation can help closed-door meetings be seen as fair. Fourth, they suggest that after the negotiation, the legislators involved should make public the larger rationale for the outcome. While we have not tested the efficacy of these detailed approaches, they provide a place to start.

The legislators at NCSL echoed some of these thoughts about better communicating decisions to compromise. One attendee wrote that legislators could avoid punishment for compromising by "informing the voters as to why the vote was cast and what would be the outcome had they voted differently" (2017 NCSL Attendee 216). Another suggested that legislators should "talk to their constituents and tell them why" (2017 NCSL Attendee 224) and a third suggested that legislators should "explain [that] incremental progress is better than none" (2017 NCSL Attendee 234). If legislators are able to lessen the downsides of holding private meetings by paying attention to these aspects of communication, it may be easier for legislators to agree to meet in private and reach more compromises.

One final point is critical; *private negotiation does not mean private lawmaking.* If everything is conducted in private and legislators hide even the final proposals from their constituents, we would not have democratic accountability. This is not our argument nor our recommendation. We must separate the process of getting to compromise from conveying the outcome of the policy agreement. Private negotiations can insulate the process from attentive voters and legislators from the fear of retribution for considering a compromise that may accompany a watchful public eye, while keeping the outcome and legislators' voting record public. Legislators can then make the case to their electorate as to why they supported the compromise policy.

7

Compromise, Voter Punishment in Primaries, and Legislative Gridlock

It is necessary and a built-in concept of the US constitution. But no candidate has ever won an election on the platform of 'I will be the best compromiser!'

2017 NCSL Attendee 145

Legislators frequently caution against letting the perfect be the enemy of the good when they are discussing policy compromises. In 1996, for example, Senator Max Baucus (D-MT) discussed his goal of repealing the gas tax but explained that he had agreed to a previous reduction by 4.3 cents per gallon and to a temporary seven-month repeal in the legislation under consideration at the time because he did not want "to let perfection be the enemy of the good" ("Congressional Record, May 2" 1996). Similarly, in 2003, Senator Bill Frist (R-TN) called on the Senate to support President George W. Bush's plan to fight AIDS. He noted that the bill was an imperfect bipartisan compromise. "But we must not let the perfect be the enemy of the good" ("Congressional Record, May 14" 2003). And in 2010, Representative Jim Costa (D-CA) called on legislators to support piecemeal immigration reform efforts, including AgJobs and the DREAM Act to permanently address DACA. He argued that "while comprehensive reform remains my priority, we cannot allow the perfect to become the enemy of the good" ("Congressional Record, June 30" 2010). The phrase "enemy of the good" appears 464 times in the Federal Congressional record from January 1995 to March of 2018.[1]

---

[1] The Congressional record is available online beginning in 1995.

The phrase "half a loaf" has been used 130 times in the same period. For example, in 2008, Senator Mary Landrieu (D-LA) explained her support for the supplemental appropriations bill by arguing that while it shortchanged some of the ongoing emergencies in her state, "I have always believed that half a loaf is better than none" ("Congressional Record, June 26" 2008). Senator Maria Cantwell (D-WA) explained her support for the 2005 energy bill, saying it "... was a bipartisan effort. I certainly know what it is like to take half a loaf. That was not the bill I would have written myself, but I voted for that legislation" ("Congressional Record, December 13" 2007). And Representative Frank Lucas (R-OK) explained his vote for the 2008 Farm Bill by noting that passing a comprehensive farm policy is critical for both producers and consumers, even if the bill fails to include all of his most preferred policies. He went on to say that farm groups back home "fear that this is the best that this body is capable of with this House leadership... I understand the fear my fellow farmers and ranchers in Oklahoma have for the future of agriculture, and at their request I will vote for this, as we would say back home in Oklahoma, 'half a loaf'" ("Congressional Record, May 14" 2008). But even as they use these words to justify votes for bills that are not perfect, not all legislators heed calls to accept half a loaf rather than holding out for the whole loaf. When legislators do not heed these calls to support compromise, the result is usually inaction, contributing to gridlock and resulting in policies that do not reflect the preferences of the legislators, or a large portion of their constituencies. In short, politics gets in the way of policy change.

REJECTING COMPROMISE, PUNISHMENT BY PRIMARY VOTERS, AND NEGOTIATING IN PRIVATE

This book has taken a problem-oriented approach to understanding how legislators' opposition to compromise contributes to gridlock and why legislators would oppose offers that give them part, but not all, of what they want. First, state legislators and city officials regularly reject proposals even when the policy content would suggest that they should prefer them to the status quo. In the first study, we presented state legislators with a proposal that was at the midpoint between the current status quo and their preferred outcome. This compromise gave them half of what they wanted without asking them to give up anything – a clear case of a half-loaf offer that all legislators should support. Yet nearly a quarter of legislators rejected this half-loaf compromise (see Chapter 2). These findings highlight an underappreciated factor – rejection of compromise – that contributes to legislative gridlock.

Second, surveys of state legislators and city officials showed that rejection of half-loaf compromise is more likely among those who fear that their constituents will punish them for compromising (see Chapter 3). This finding highlights the importance of legislators' perceptions of their constituents for understanding how the electoral connection shapes legislator behavior, and the tension legislators may face between their electoral and policy goals. Legislators' fear is centered upon punishment from primary voters. Consistent with this concern, Republican incumbents during the period 2011–2015 were more likely to vote against compromise bills when there were more Tea Party supporters in their district (see Chapter 4). Since Tea Party support predicts rejection of compromise when controlling for the ideology of the district, and even the ideology of strong co-partisans in the district, this indicates that the primary electorate shapes legislative outcomes in ways that are not reflected in ideology.

As we have shown, only a subset of primary voters punish compromise, and most voters reward, rather than punish, compromise (see Chapter 5). However, the primary voters who opposed the specific compromise in a survey experiment did punish the legislator if she voted for it. This group represents about one-third of the primary electorate in our study and these voters punish compromise despite the fact that they were getting half of what they wanted without having to give anything up. Because these voters may care deeply about the issue on which the legislator compromised, and may provide support to mobilize a primary challenger, and the number of voters who might punish the legislator may accumulate across many compromise votes the legislator takes, legislators have incentives to seriously consider the threat of punishment for compromising.

While rejection of compromise may be a logical choice for legislators who face uncertainty about which compromise votes may prove electorally damaging, this behavior raises concerns about representation. Legislators who reject half-loaf compromises appear to be representing the vocal minority at the expense of the vast majority of constituents who favor compromise. A 2018 interview with Senator John McCain (R-AZ) further highlights this problem and the need for citizens who support compromise to become more active, giving legislators more reason to listen to their views. Senator McCain argued that, if individual voters lament the lack of civility and compromise in politics, then they must do something about it:

Because I guarantee you, voters on the Far Right and Far Left are. If you want politics to be more civil, if you want Congress to argue less and get more done, then show up. Represent. Play as big a role in the mundane activities of politics as the zealots do. It's important. (Montanaro 2018)

Barring the change in participation John McCain called for, there may be other ways to increase the likelihood of reaching a compromise and overcoming gridlock. Taking the threat of voter punishment in primaries seriously represents an important avenue for evaluating what negotiation processes may promote more compromise. The experiments in Chapter 6 show that legislators believed they were more likely to reach a compromise solution if negotiations were held in private. When legislators can avoid the pressures to posture and save face before a public audience, they may be more willing to consider a compromise and the concessions it would entail. This finding highlights how institutional rules and norms interact with legislators' electoral considerations.

Based on these findings, we argue that legislators' belief that primary voters punish compromise contributes to the problem of gridlock. This perception manifests in legislators voting against proposals that they acknowledge they prefer, and even when their stated preference incorporates overall voter preferences. When added to a polarized political environment, in which parties want to move policy in opposite directions on many issues, legislators' rejection of compromises that give them some, but not all, of what they want makes it all the more difficult to address the problems confronting the country, states, and localities. Despite the benefits of compromising for advancing legislation and moving policy toward individual legislators' induced policy preferences, these compromises may be at odds with legislators' perceived electoral incentives. As Senators Trent Lott (R-MS) and Tom Daschle (D-SD) have noted, partisan issues are often a safety zone, while "the risky places are in the middle: compromising positions, reaching halfway, making deals with the other side. ... It's easier to raise money and rally your base as a soldier in the fight than as a dealer at the table" (Lott and Daschle 2017, 42).

THE SHADOW OF VOTER PUNISHMENT IN
PRIMARIES DURING THE 1986 TAX REFORM

In this book we have shown that one cause of inaction is fear that primary voters will punish legislators who compromise. We have described many instances when legislators failed to compromise because of their fear of electoral punishment. The story of the 1986 tax reform is an example where legislators were able to reach a compromise, and its lesson aligns with many of our core findings about both the challenges to compromise and the potential remedies.

On October 22, 1986, President Ronald Reagan signed into law an overhaul of the tax code that had been nearly three years in the making. An op-ed in the *New York Times* remarked that "[f]or years to come, students of politics will look to the odyssey of the new tax law as a prime example of how the American system of government gets things done" (Rosenbaum 1986). The president had signaled his desire to pass a tax reform in his January 1984 State of the Union address. In the address, Reagan indicated that he would ask the Treasury Department to develop a proposal to be delivered to Congress after the November elections. True to that request, the Treasury released a plan in late November. The plan went nowhere. Legislators from both parties disliked it. The broad idea in the Treasury's plan was to reduce overall tax rates but offset these changes by closing loopholes in the tax code. This was unpopular because the targeted loopholes benefited businesses ranging from cattle feed lots to banks, as well as individual voters.

Further negotiations led to a second Treasury plan that maintained many more loopholes than the first. President Reagan launched the new effort with a May 28 speech to the nation arguing for tax reform even in the face of interest group opposition to the elimination of loopholes, saying "Tax relief is in sight. Let's make it a reality. Let's not let prisoners of mediocrity wear us down. Let's not let the special interest raids of the few rob us of all of our dreams" (Birnbaum and Murray 1987, 95). The Chair of the House Ways and Means Committee, Representative Dan Rostenkowski (D-IL), spoke next and also supported reform. He was not from the president's party, but he saw an opportunity for Democrats to gain some credit for tax reform as well.

The effort faced major opposition from lobbyists and members of Congress whose constituents enjoyed some of the tax loopholes then in place. As with the 2017 tax reforms, deductions for state and local taxes were a point of contention. High-tax states viewed the deductions as critical so that their taxpayers would not be unequally burdened and would continue to support investments in the state and local communities. The Coalition Against Double Taxation – one group advocating to keep these deductions – adopted a no compromise strategy, in which they refused to endorse a bill that allowed any decrease in state and local deductions. Despite this opposition, the bill Rostenkowski initially introduced preserved only some of the tax deductions. It faced immediate opposition.

Rostenkowski began closed-door markup sessions to amend the bill, while lobbyists gathered outside in the hallways. The amendments slowly reopened loopholes, eventually approving a major tax break for banks that opened the door to so many tax breaks that real reform appeared to be dead. Rostenkowski, having interviewed each member of Congress to assess which tax breaks were most important to their constituents, started over and slowly built a coalition in favor of reform by agreeing to keep some of these critical tax breaks while cutting others. The final deal-making occurred during a closed-door weekend session and the committee approved the bill. After intense lobbying by President Reagan, the committee bill passed the House of Representatives.

Yet efforts at tax reform faced the same difficult path in the Senate because of concerns over cutting too many of the deductions that voters wanted. In fact, Senator and Committee Chair Bob Packwood (R-OR) introduced a bill to the Finance Committee that had more tax breaks than what was included in the bill the House had passed. The committee amended the bill to include even more deductions. Ultimately, Packwood allowed the committee to adjourn, rather than pass a bill that could not really be called tax reform.

Packwood revived the tax reform effort with a proposal to slash individual rates and eliminate nearly all tax breaks. After Packwood announced to the press and lobbyists that there would be no sessions over the weekend, key senators met in secret to finalize the proposal. Packwood and some members of his committee had worked "privately, out of the public eye" to generate a reform plan that was "even more radical than the one passed by the Democratic House: a plan that cuts back a wide swath of special-interest tax breaks and lowers the top statutory tax rate to 27 percent" according to *Wall Street Journal* reporters who followed the story closely (Birnbaum and Murray 1987, 5). Following closed-door sessions that week, the committee passed the bill unanimously. Because of a rule that required any amendments to be revenue-neutral, any restoration of tax breaks by amendments on the Senate floor would have had to be paired with increased tax rates. The committee bill passed the Senate (97–3) without major amendments.

The conference committee process was arduous, but the two chairmen eventually returned with a bill that largely eliminated the tax loopholes and lowered tax rates. It passed in the House of Representatives 292–136 and in the Senate 74–23. Legislators delivered on the promise of tax reform. In this case, as in many instances of policy reform, compromise was critical. Successful policy change nearly always requires legislators to make compromises and to accept part of what they want even if they cannot get everything they want.

Many of the dynamics that we find drive a lack of compromise were at play in the 1986 tax reform efforts, but policy advocates were able to overcome the initial opposition to compromise and reach an agreement. First, consider the initial opposition to compromise by legislators. Although both Democrats and Republicans were, in principle, in favor of tax reform that included lower rates paired with a reduction in tax breaks, individual legislators rejected the compromise proposals. Packwood said of the members of his committee, "I discovered that if they have priorities one, two, and three, and you give them one, two, and three, then four, five, and six become their most important priorities" (Birnbaum and Murray 1987, 198–99). These legislators appeared to reject half a loaf because they wanted the whole loaf.

The fear of punishment appears to have mattered in the case of the 1986 tax reforms as well. Legislators deciding how to vote on the tax reforms worried that their constituents would oppose the likely concessions in any compromise. Even Packwood's first bill included tax breaks for the timber industry, a key economic force in his home state of Oregon, and a group that he did not want to anger. And groups such as the Coalition Against Double Taxation organized to oppose compromise on deductions for state and local taxes. Senator George Mitchell (D-ME), who had a policy of meeting with any constituents who asked, scheduled numerous 15-minute meetings each day to hear constituents' complaints about the tax bill. These meetings, which started in the afternoon, often ran late into the evening (Birnbaum and Murray 1987). At the end of a long day of meetings with constituents, Senator Mitchell said "It follows a predictable pattern. They all want 100 percent" (Birnbaum and Murray 1987, 198). It was clear that voters opposed many aspects of the proposed compromise, which likely made legislators wary.

Yet, policymakers were able to overcome opposition to compromise and reach a deal. They did this by using private negotiations. The committees resorted to convening in private no less than three times during the 1986 negotiations. In the House, they met in a closed-door weekend session to hammer out the final compromise bill. In the Senate, a few key members met in secret to develop a final proposal for the committee over a weekend after having specifically, and publicly, promised no action on the bill. And House Committee Chair Rostenkowski met in private with Senate Committee Chair Packwood to develop a compromise conference proposal reconciling differences between the House and the Senate, rather than publicly meeting with the whole conference committee (Birnbaum and Murray 1987). Meeting in private allowed policymakers to identify acceptable concessions without having to worry about posturing before key groups of constituents. Legislators then presented the final deal to their voters and made the case for their support of the legislation.

While the 1986 tax reform provides an example of a successful compromise, our research highlights how perceptions of electoral backlash for compromising can lead legislators to reject half-loaf compromises that benefit them, contributing to gridlock in the process. We now turn to the broader implications of these findings in three areas: legislators' home style and their communication with constituents; primary elections; and gridlock – the concern that motivated this research.

LEGISLATIVE HOME STYLE

The threat of punishment by primary voters is a significant obstacle to achieving more compromise, so solutions for overcoming gridlock that adapt to or accommodate that threat are more likely to be successful. In Chapter 6, we showed that holding negotiations in private can be a successful strategy. Yet, if this approach is pursued, reformers should be attentive to concerns about representation and accountability. Even while better insulating the negotiating process, legislators should be transparent about the final compromise, communicating it and explaining it to their constituents. As we concluded in Chapter 6, if the entirety of legislating occurs in private and voters have no information about how their representatives voted, the damage to representative democracy could be even worse than the problems stemming from gridlock. This suggests that any reforms should still ensure that constituents learn about policy outcomes and legislators' votes.

Communication can be important for democratic accountability and may also limit the likelihood of voter punishment in primaries. In the open-ended portion of the survey at the 2017 NCSL meeting, we asked the legislators and staff, "Is there anything else legislators can do to avoid being punished by voters when they support compromise bills?" The most common response, given by more than 80% (153 out of 188), was that legislators could do a better job communicating with constituents. They wrote things like:

Explain their vote/reasoning. (2017 NCSL Attendee 1)

Clear messaging as to the alternatives. (2017 NCSL Attendee 9)

Get ahead of the oppositions' PR to frame the vote as the right + ethical thing to do for the district. (2017 NCSL Attendee 13)

Knock on doors. 1-on-1 talks can be disarming & therefore educational. (2017 NCSL Attendee 62)

Be loyal to their principles & communicate well with their constituents. (2017 NCSL Attendee 76)

Try to explain in the media. (2017 NCSL Attendee 86)

Communicate. (2017 NCSL Attendee 90)

Speak to them directly. Help them understand why they voted the way they did. (2017 NCSL Attendee 102)

Be proactive in explaining vote for compromise. (2017 NCSL Attendee 192)

They should be able and have a relationship with their district to be able to explain their reasoning behind their vote. (2017 NCSL Attendee 193)

Get their side of the story out through constit[uent] meetings, newsletters, email. (2017 NCSL Attendee 208)

Explain incremental progress is better than none. (2017 NCSL Attendee 234)

One important question is what form this communication should take. While the legislators and staff consistently pointed to legislative communication as a key solution, there are many things that legislators could focus on in this effort. One option is to build support for the policy compromise itself. This might involve explaining why incremental progress is better than none or how the compromise represents an important victory. Congressman Jose Serrano (D-NY) explained his yes vote on the 2016 Puerto Rico Oversight, Management, and Economic Stability Act in a newsletter to his constituents by noting that, while he had reservations about some provisions of the compromise bill, there was no other realistic alternative:

Simply put, it is either this bill, with its flaws, or nothing. Doing nothing will only lead to the crisis getting worse. Vulture funds will file lawsuits that could take further funding away from essential programs and services in Puerto Rico. The public pension system will go broke within three years, and will have no protections in court battles. The economic situation will only get worse for millions of Puerto Ricans. (Serrano 2016)

Recent field experiments on political communication have shown that legislators have a limited ability to change constituents' opinion on an issue. In a meta-analysis of 49 experiments on persuasion, the effectiveness of efforts to persuade voters depended on the partisan context (Kalla and Broockman 2017). Where there was a strong partisan signal (such as in general elections with competing partisan candidates), messaging had no impact on voters' intended vote choice. Where partisan signals were less strong (such as in primary elections and ballot initiatives), messaging had a small persuasive effect (see also Grose et al. 2015; Broockman and Butler 2017). This may mean that legislators can persuade their co-partisan primary voters to not punish compromise. Even small shifts among these voters who might otherwise punish could protect legislators enough to assuage their worries about voting for compromise. On the other hand, when voters care deeply about an issue, their views may be resistant to change (Krosnick 1990), suggesting that they may be less open to legislators' efforts to communicate the benefits of compromise.

Given the limitations they face in persuading voters to agree with them, a second option for legislators is to focus on messaging and communications strategies that provide them with the leeway to vote for a position even if it is unpopular. In other words, legislators might use their communication to build trust that leads voters to continue to support them even if they vote for a specific compromise that the voters oppose (Bianco 1994). In this case, the communication would not necessarily always be about the compromise proposal; rather, it would include information about how the legislator approaches issues, seeks to represent constituents, and aims to address important problems.

Focusing on messaging strategies that give the legislator more leeway to support compromises represents a promising, though undertested, alternative. Fenno (1978) noted that spending time in the district was a major part of a legislator's job and he referred to this work as being a legislator's "home style." Legislators' home style reflects how they present themselves to voters, how they allocate their resources, and how they explain their activities in Washington. While a legislator's home style could take various forms, one goal of these efforts is to build trust with constituents to gain leeway for the times when they vote in ways contrary to their constituents' preferences. One way of building trust is through communicating about actions taken in the legislature. Indeed, Fenno (1978, 141) and Kingdon (1973, 46–53) suggest that legislators are wary of casting a vote when they are worried about how to explain their position. Using time spent in the district to build trust may facilitate such explanations. A related approach may be to use their communication to present themselves to constituents as hard-working, thoughtful legislators who are trying to make the right decision for the district and broader community.

If such efforts sway co-partisans who oppose particular compromises, legislators may be able to use that leeway to support more compromise solutions.

A few of the 2017 NCSL attendees explicitly noted that building trust should be the goal of communication. For example, one attendee wrote that legislators could avoid being punished by voters with "strong constituent engagement to ensure the electorate feels connected to the legislator" (2017 NCSL Attendee 80). Another wrote that legislators should "[e]ducate their constituents and gain their trust for their judgment" (2017 NCSL Attendee 11). Still another attendee wrote "build trust w/yr constituents. Spend *a lot* of time with them and be able and willing to explain yourself when you disagree" (2017 NCSL Attendee 210).

One of the most promising routes for building trust *and* persuading voters is the online deliberative town hall model (Neblo et al. 2010; Esterling et al. 2011). A representative sample of constituents are invited to participate in these forums and they are given the chance to ask questions of their legislators and hear the members' responses. The results of experiments on this form of communication are encouraging – voters want to know what the legislator thought and why, voters who attended moderated their positions in response to good arguments from the legislator, and voters' trust in the legislator increased. Moreover, the effects of trust and other favorable evaluations of the legislator endure even several months after a town hall. If legislators engage in this form of deliberative town hall regularly, they can build up trust among many constituents, possibly giving them leeway to support compromise. And when compromises are on the agenda, they could bring their rationale to their constituents and seek to persuade voters to support the compromise.

It is especially important to understand how legislators can earn leeway from the voters in their primary electorate. While legislators rely on support from all types of voters, the primary voters who oppose compromise are the ones who punish. If legislators can cultivate trust among their primary voters, then they may not fear electoral retribution for supporting compromises, which in turn may make it easier to reach legislative agreements to solve important problems.

PRIMARY ELECTIONS

Our research shows that legislators are concerned about the negative backlash to compromise from the primary electorate. We argue that legislators' perception that primary voters punish compromise, and their responsiveness to this segment of the electorate, contributes to gridlock in ways that have been previously overlooked. Legislators' attentiveness to the perceived opposition to compromise from this segment of the electorate also affects which voters are well represented by their elected leaders. Legislators may alter their behavior to align with the primary electorate rather than the general electorate, causing them to take positions that are more extreme than what the general electorate wants (Burden 2001; Brady et al. 2007) or to reject particular policy compromises opposed by part of their primary electorate.

Even a subset of the primary electorate can be influential. A small group of activists in the electorate can highlight a legislator's perceived shortcomings and pave the way for a primary challenger. Strong challengers are strategic in joining the fray (Jacobson and Kernell 1983; Carson et al. 2012), and discontent among a vocal minority of the electorate over a legislator's support for compromise may provide challengers the opening they seek.

Voters who care deeply about a given issue are important for understanding legislators' behavior. Beyond the geographic, reelection, primary, and personal constituencies that Fenno (1978) highlights, legislators face an electorate that is also fractured on the basis of issues. And those who oppose compromise on a particular issue punish legislators who compromise with lower approval and a lower likelihood of voting for them. Moreover, there may be many such groups of voters who oppose compromise on different issues. These "issue public" voters who care deeply about a given issue gather more information about the issue (Iyengar et al. 2008) and engage in more activism (see e.g., Krosnick et al. 1994). It is no wonder then that legislators fear their influence in lower-turnout primary elections.

Asking how open versus closed primaries affect legislator positions (McGhee et al. 2014) or whether top-two primaries reduce polarization (Ahler et al. 2016; McGhee and Shor 2017) answers only part of the question about how primary elections shape political outcomes. Legislators' perceptions of primary voters – across various institutional environments – also matter. Our research highlights the importance of legislators' perceptions of their constituents and their beliefs that primary voters oppose compromise.

One question that our findings raise is whether changes in the primary electorate over time have made legislators more fearful of punishment and therefore less likely to compromise. Although we cannot answer this question directly from our own study, there is suggestive evidence that primary voters may have become more ideological and thus more likely to oppose compromise. Consider patterns of ideology in the public. On average, voters with more extreme ideology do not punish their legislator for compromising. But extreme ideology does predict being in the smaller slice of the primary electorate – those who oppose a particular compromise – that does punish compromise (see Chapter 5). To be clear, ideological extremists are not the only voters who punish compromise, but ideological extremity is the one demographic predictor of punishment. As such, voter ideology provides an indirect way to explore whether legislators might worry about punishment more now than in the past. In the 1972 American National Election Study, only 3.8% of respondents identified as extremely liberal or conservative (Hutchings et al. 2018). By 2016, this had doubled to 7.3% of respondents. Though primary voters have long been more ideological than the average citizen, we observe a similar increase over time in ideological extremity among self-identified primary voters. Among voters in the 1972 presidential primary, 5.8% identified as extremely liberal or conservative, compared to 11% in 2016 (Hutchings et al. 2017, 2018). Moreover, legislators appear to recognize this ideological disparity between primary and general election voters. In a 2002 survey by Carey et al. (2002), state legislators viewed the average Democratic primary voter as significantly more ideologically extreme than the average general election voter (mean of 1.1 for Democratic primary, mean of 0.88 for general; $p < 0.001$, two-sided on a folded scale from moderate = 0 to most liberal/conservative = 3). The average Republican primary voter was viewed as even more ideological (mean of 1.6 for Republican primary, mean of 0.88 for general, $p < 0.001$, two-sided). Since ideological extremity is a predictor of opposing the various compromises offered to the legislator in Chapter 5, an increase in ideological extremity suggests that there may be more primary voters who are willing to punish the legislator for supporting a half-loaf compromise now than in the past.

While the likelihood an incumbent member of Congress will face a primary challenger has not increased dramatically over the past four decades (Boatright 2013) and relatively few incumbents lose in primary elections, there are several possible reasons legislators' concern about primary elections may have grown over time. These reasons go beyond voter ideology and point to the importance of legislators' perceptions. The first is that high profile losses may make legislators concerned about the risk of losing. They may be thinking "if Majority Leader Cantor can lose in a primary, surely I can too." The second reason legislators may be increasingly concerned with engaged segments of the primary electorate is that these voters could help fund a primary challenger. Indeed, recent ideological challengers raise substantially more money from individual donors than they have in past decades (Boatright 2013). The third reason legislators may view primary elections as more important to winning and maintaining a legislative seat is increased sorting of partisanship and ideology among the public (Levendusky 2009; Mason 2015), along with geographic sorting (Nall 2015). When voters are loyal to a single party in congressional and presidential elections, and when district boundaries create increasingly safe partisan districts where the majority of voters regularly vote for one party (Abramowitz 2010; Harbridge 2015), few congressional races are competitive in the general election. In 2018, for example, Ballotpedia predicted that only 38 of the 435 races for the US House of Representatives (8.7%) would be truly competitive in the general election. A similar pattern holds for state legislative races. In both cases, this can shift competition to the primary election. Combined with rising polarization in state and federal politics (Shor and McCarty 2011; Rigby and Wright 2015; Grumbach 2018), greater fear of punishment from primary voters and rejection of compromise could contribute to the rising gridlock on a range of policies.

Another question is whether concerns about primary challengers and the fear of voter retribution for compromise is higher among Republicans than Democrats. No organized effort against compromise on the Democratic side has matched the Tea Party movement as of yet, and some evidence from both voters and legislators suggests that there may be a partisan difference in opposition to compromise at present. For instance, in a postelection interview, the 2016 American National Election Study asked respondents whether they agreed or disagreed with the statement that compromise in politics is selling out on one's principles. Among Republicans, ideological extremity (a factor that is also related to being a primary voter) is positively related to agreeing that compromise is selling out ($p < 0.001$, two-sided), but the same is not true among Democrats (Hutchings et al. 2017).

Among our findings, both the survey results and the open-ended comments from state legislators at the 2017 NCSL (see Chapter 4) also suggest stronger opposition to compromise among Republican voters. While both Democrats and Republicans feared retribution from primary voters, Republicans believed their primary voters were significantly more vengeful than Democratic primary voters. Legislators' open-ended comments reiterated this concern, with legislators suggesting that concerns were particularly acute on the Republican side. One attendee provided several examples of Republicans who faced retribution for compromising: "4 Republican legislators voted for a compromise transportation bill that raised the gas tax. One didn't run again, one was defeated in the primary, one barely won, and the 4th changed parties to become a Democrat" (2017 NCSL Attendee 260). After giving several examples of Republicans who compromised and subsequently lost in primary elections in the early 2000s, in 2015, and 2016, one legislator noted, "[I] can't think of any D examples" (2017 NCSL Attendee 92). Overall, this suggests that there may be some differences in how primary electorates on the left and right respond to compromise. Whether this reflects anything inherent about the importance of principles and ideology to Republicans (Grossmann and Hopkins 2015), or simply reflects a political moment when Republicans were the minority during the Obama presidency, remains to be seen.

Some anecdotes indicate that Democrats have also faced backlash for compromise in recent years. After Democrats became the minority party following the 2016 presidential election, several long-serving incumbents faced primary challengers in 2018 who argued that the incumbent representatives were too moderate and too willing to compromise. Senator Dianne Feinstein (D-CA), for example, failed to get the endorsement from her party during California's annual Democratic Party convention. Party activists favored her progressive rival – state Senator Kevin de Leon – by a margin of 54–37, with neither candidate receiving the 60 votes needed for endorsement (Siders and Marinucci 2018). More generally, Feinstein has faced pressure from Democratic activists because of her willingness to compromise and work with Republicans. Speaking at the Public Policy Institute of California, Feinstein argued that compromise is what is needed to get things done. She said, "I know where I want to go and how to get as close to that as possible ... without compromising on anything major." Channeling what many activists seem to feel, someone in the crowd yelled, "It's all major" (Wildermuth 2017).

In Illinois, Representative Dan Lipinski (D-IL) also faced a tough primary challenge in 2018. Lipinski is a moderate Democrat serving an area that covers some of suburbs around Chicago. Although he has served for fourteen years, his victory over Marie Newman, whose campaign accused him of being too conservative, was narrow. In evaluating Newman's challenge, Lipinski accused Newman and her supporters of being a "Tea Party of the left," saying that their assault against moderation would hurt the Democratic party and add to gridlock in Congress (Associated Press 2018).

While Feinstein and Lipinski both won, Representatives Joseph Crowley (D-NY) and Mike Capuano (D-MA) were not so lucky in 2018. Both Crowley and Capuano were long-standing incumbents who lost to

primary challengers who were more liberal. Crowley lost to Alexandra
Ocasio-Cortez and Capuano lost to Ayanna Pressley. Crowley's defeat
was particularly striking; it was the first time he faced a primary challenger since 2004 and he heavily outspent Ocasio-Cortez. He was
also a high-ranking Democrat who was viewed as a contender for the
Speakership in the next few years. His record was liberal, but Alexandria
Ocasio-Cortez ran on the need to have even more progressive representation in Washington.

Other Democratic incumbents may decide to move to the left to avoid
tough primary challenges like those from Ocasio-Cortez and Pressley in
the coming years, much as some Republican legislators like Senator Orrin
Hatch (R-UT) did after seeing Tea Party candidates defeat their colleagues
(see Karol 2015, 76). Representative Ocasio-Cortez (D-NY) made waves
within in her own party during her first weeks in Congress by threatening to back primary opponents against other Democratic members she
deems as too moderate (Bade and Caygle 2019). And this threat may have
some teeth, as many Democratic voters appear willing to support potential primary challengers. A 2018 poll found that a majority of Democratic
voters agreed with the statement that "Democrats should provide a clear,
positive agenda to contrast with Trump and the Republican culture of
corruption. Primary elections ensure the strongest Democrats emerge to
advance that agenda" (Rojas and Mcelwee 2019). This growing fear of
primary challengers may be enough to keep many Democratic incumbents from considering compromise proposals in the future.

GRIDLOCK

We began this book with a focus on the pervasive and problematic gridlock facing both the US Congress and many state legislatures. Legislative
gridlock is a frequent and often bemoaned aspect of the American policymaking process (see e.g., Mayhew 1991; Binder 2003; Burden 2011;
Gutmann and Thompson 2012). It has led to failures to address immigration, long-term plans for infrastructure, gun violence, climate change,
reforms to entitlement programs, and budgetary planning, among others. Our findings about rejection of half-loaf compromises both highlight an overlooked source of gridlock and point to a way forward on
overcoming gridlock.

While polarization and heightened partisanship have clearly contributed to gridlock, and there are many issue areas in which Democrats and
Republicans want to move policy in opposite directions, the fact that

legislators frequently reject proposals that move policy in their direction because they reject compromise adds further challenges. Legislators who reject half-loaf compromises make it more difficult to gather the votes necessary to pass legislation. In some of the examples we presented, the rejection of compromise affected the ability of the majority party to hold together their members in support of policy change. In others, the rejection of compromise broke apart bipartisan deals. The rates of rejection of half-loaf compromises we observed are consequential for policy outcomes. If 23% of legislators (the fraction of state legislators who rejected the halfway offer in our gas tax study) reject a half-loaf compromise in the House of Representatives where passage of a bill requires 218 votes, this would mean that passage would require that 283 (i.e., 218/77%) members of Congress view the bill as closer to their preferred outcome then the status quo. Some of those 283 would be expected to the reject the bill, so passing a compromise with a bare majority would require a bill to bring policy closer to a supermajority of legislators. This rejection of half-loaf compromises exacerbates gridlock.

Our results show that legislators' rejection of compromise is tied to their perception that primary voters will punish them for compromising. Although the public generally supports compromise, we observe that the threat of retribution can arise among the voters who oppose a specific compromise proposal. Legislators may expect that a group of primary voters might mobilize on any given issue even when the proposal appears to move policy closer to what the legislator and voters want. Across their term in office, a given legislator may expect to face uncompromising co-partisans in their district on many different issues, and these punishing voters may be different on the many compromise votes legislators face, meaning that they add up to more than the one-third of primary voters we identify on a given vote in our survey. These voters' potential impact in primary elections, combined with the risk that their opposition could fuel a stronger primary challenger, is likely to cause many legislators to act cautiously and reject compromise. Following Representative Lipinski's narrow primary victory in 2018, the executive director of No Labels co-wrote an op-ed for the *Wall Street Journal* that decried the threat that legislators who compromise can face in the primary:

Legislators in both parties have to worry too much about primary challenges from ideologues on the far left or far right. That's why Democrats and Republicans are so unwilling to work across the aisle. And that in turn is why Congress is failing to address the biggest problems facing America. (White and Borowsky 2018)

These dynamics are one more obstacle to passing legislation in a system already designed to make changing the status quo difficult.

Our evidence points toward a set of reforms for passing more compromise solutions: taking steps to reduce the opportunities for a small group of committed primary voters to shape legislators' behavior. As we have shown, one way to increase legislators' willingness to accept compromise is to insulate the process of negotiation from the public. Legislators expect that privately held negotiations are more likely to yield compromise solutions. Private negotiations have the advantage of protecting legislators from revealing what they are willing to give up in the compromise until they can also reveal what they have gained. Because the voters in the survey in Chapter 5 who opposed the specific compromise opposed it even when it did not provide information about the concessions on any other dimension, such a process is unlikely to fully mitigate their opposition. Instead, it may serve to limit the ability of the groups who oppose the compromise to mobilize opposition on the basis of the concessions. It may also allow legislators to thoughtfully consider compromise offers without worry about posturing to an audience. This insulation from the public does not mean that public accountability and the transparency of voting records should be abandoned. Legislators who support compromises must still face the electorate and no structure of the bargaining processes should keep the electorate from learning about and evaluating legislators' ultimate actions.

In addition to insulating the process of negotiations from the public, any solutions that build support for compromise among primary voters are potential ways to improve the prospects for legislative compromise. The improved communication that legislators emphasize is one such solution. If voters who would oppose compromise can be convinced to support it, or if the rest of the public that overwhelmingly supports compromise can be mobilized, legislators could more easily vote for half-loaf compromises.

Solving many of today's pressing problems requires that legislators from different perspectives find and support compromise solutions. A key factor in preventing many legislators from supporting compromise solutions is the fear of punishment by their primary voters. To mitigate the fear of punishment in primaries, political processes and institutions should be put in place that give legislators more distance from these voters during the negotiation phase. In a world that needs more common ground solutions, implementing procedures that will increase the likelihood of reaching compromise is a good place to start.

References

Abramowitz, Alan I. 2010. *The Disappearing Center.* New Haven: Yale University Press.

2012. "Grand Old Tea Party: Partisan Polarization and the Rise of the Tea Party Movement." In *Steep: The Precipitous Rise of the Tea Party,* eds. Lawrence Rosenthal and Christine Trost. Berkeley: University of California Press.

Adams, James, Samuel Merrill III, Elizabeth N. Simas, and Walter J. Stone. 2011. "When Candidates Value Good Character: A Spatial Model with Applications to Congressional Elections." *The Journal of Politics* 73 (1): 17–30.

Ahler, Douglas J., Jack Citrin, and Gabriel S. Lenz. 2016. "Do Open Primaries Improve Representation? An Experimental Test of California's 2012 Top-Two Primary." *Legislative Studies Quarterly* 41 (2): 237–68.

Anderson, Sarah E., Daniel M. Butler, and Laurel Harbridge. 2016. "Legislative Institutions as a Source of Party Leaders' Influence." *Legislative Studies Quarterly* 41 (3): 605–31.

"Another moderate shown the door." 2012. *The Economist,* May 12, 2012. [cited April 10, 2018]. Available from www.economist.com/the-economist-explains/2013/09/04/why-are-the-economists-writers-anonymous.

Ansolabehere, Stephen. 2012. "CCES Common Content, 2010." hdl:1902.1/17705, Harvard Dataverse, V3.

Ansolabehere, Stephen, and Brian Schaffner. 2013. "CCES Common Content, 2012." hdl:1902.1/21447, Harvard Dataverse, V8.

Ansolabehere, Stephen, James M. Snyder, and Michael M. Ting. 2003. "Bargaining in Bicameral Legislatures: When and Why Does Malapportionment Matter?" *American Political Science Review* 97 (3): 471–81.

Anzia, Sarah F., and Molly C. Jackman. 2013. "Legislative Organization and the Second Face of Power: Evidence from U.S. State Legislatures." *The Journal of Politics* 75 (1): 210–24.

Arnold, R. Douglas. 1990. *The Logic of Congressional Action.* New Haven, CT: Yale University Press.

Associated Press. 2017. "Illinois Senate overrides Gov. Rauner's budget veto." *Associated Press,* July 4, 2017. [cited July 6, 2017]. Available from www.dailyherald.com/business/20170704/illinois-senate-overrides-rauners-budget-vetoes.

    2018. "Rep. Dan Lipinski narrowly beats Marie Newman in Illinois Democratic primary." *NBC News,* March 21, 2018. [cited March 26, 2018]. Available from www.nbcnews.com/politics/congress/rep-dan-lipinski-narrowly-beats-marie-newman-illinois-democratic-primary-n858571.

Bade, Rachael, and Heather Caygle. 2019. "Exasperated Democrats try to rein in Ocasio-Cortez." *Politico,* January 11, 2019. [cited January 25, 2019]. Available from www.politico.com/story/2019/01/11/alexandria-ocasio-cortez-democrats-establisment-1093728.

Bai, Matt. 2012. "Obama vs. Boehner: Who killed the debt deal?" *The New York Times Magazine,* March 28, 2012. [cited September 5, 2017]. Available from www.nytimes.com/2012/04/01/magazine/obama-vs-boehner-who-killed-the-debt-deal.html?mcubz=0.

Bailey, Michael A., Jonathan Mummolo, and Hans Noel. 2012. "Tea Party Influence." *American Politics Research* 40 (5): 769–804.

Baker, Ross K. 2015. *Is Bipartisanship Dead? A Report from the Senate.* Boulder, CO: Paradigm Publishers.

Ballotpedia. 2014a. *Partisan Composition of State Houses.* [cited July 31, 2014]. Available from http://ballotpedia.org/Partisan_composition_of_state_houses.

    2014b. *Partisan Composition of State Senates.* [cited July 31, 2014]. Available from http://ballotpedia.org/Partisan_composition_of_state_senates.

    2014c. *State Legislatures with Term Limits.* [cited July 31, 2014]. Available from http://ballotpedia.org/State_legislatures_with_term_limits.

    2016a. *Incumbents with a Primary Challenger in the 2016 State Legislative Elections.* [cited March 18, 2019]. Available from https://ballotpedia.org/Incumbents_with_a_primary_challenger_in_the_2016_state_legislative_elections.

    2016b. *State Legislative Elections.* [cited August 18, 2017]. Available from https://ballotpedia.org/State_legislative_elections.

    2016c. *U.S. House Primaries.* [cited August 18, 2017]. Available from https://ballotpedia.org/U.S._House_primaries.

Barber, Michael J. 2016. "Ideological Donors, Contribution Limits, and the Polarization of American Legislatures." *The Journal of Politics* 78 (1): 296–310.

Barker, Rocky. 2016. "Land-transfer agitator Chmelik loses in Idaho County." *Idaho Statesman,* May 19, 2016. [cited January 4, 2018]. Available from www.idahostatesman.com/news/local/news-columns-blogs/letters-from-the-west/article78731237.html

Baron, David P., and John A. Ferejohn. 1989. "Bargaining in Legislatures." *American Political Science Review* 83 (4): 1181–206.

Bartels, Larry M. 2000. "Partisanship and Voting Behavior: 1952–1996." *American Journal of Political Science* 44 (1): 35–50.

Bauer, Nichole M., Laurel Harbridge Yong, and Yanna Krupnikov. 2017. "Who Is Punished? Conditions Affecting Voter Evaluations of Legislators Who Do Not Compromise." *Political Behavior* 39 (2): 279–300.

Baumgartner, Frank R., Jeffrey M. Berry, Marie Hojnacki, David C. Kimball, and Beth L. Leech. 2009. *Lobbying and Policy Change: Who Wins, Who Loses, and Why.* Chicago, IL: University of Chicago Press.

Bawn, Kathleen, Martin Cohen, David Karol, Seth Masket, Hans Noel, and John Zaller. 2012. "A Theory of Political Parties: Groups, Policy Demands and Nominations in American Politics." *Perspectives on Politics* 10 (3): 571–97.

Bennis, Will M., Douglas L. Medin, and Daniel M. Bartels. 2010. "The Costs and Benefits of Calculation and Moral Rules." *Perspectives on Psychological Science* 5 (2): 187–202.

Berman, Russell. 2015. "Paul Ryan's Uneasy Alliance with the House Freedom Caucus." *The Atlantic*, October 22, 2015. [cited December 19, 2017]. Available from www.theatlantic.com/politics/archive/2015/10/paul-ryans-uneasy-alliance-with-the-house-freedom-caucus/411715/.

Bertelli, Anthony M., and Christian R. Grose. 2006. "The Spatial Model and the Senate Trial of President Clinton." *American Politics Research* 34 (4): 535–59.

Bianco, William T. 1994. *Trust: Representatives and Constituents.* Ann Arbor, MI: University of Michigan Press.

Binder, Sarah. 2003. *Stalemate: Causes and Consequences of Legislative Gridlock.* Washington, DC: Brookings Institution Press.

2014. "Polarized We Govern?" Washington, DC: Brookings Institution Press.

2015. "Can Paul Ryan disarm the Freedom Caucus?" *The Washington Post*, October 25, 2015. [cited December 19, 2017]. Available from www.washingtonpost.com/news/monkey-cage/wp/2015/10/26/can-paul-ryan-disarm-the-freedom-caucus/?utm_term=.03af4621fe66.

Binder, Sarah A., and Frances E. Lee. 2016. "Making Deals in Congress." In *Political Negotiation*, ed. J. Mansbridge and C. J. Martin. Washington, DC: Brookings. pp. 91–117.

Binning, Kevin R., David K. Sherman, Geoffrey L. Cohen, and Kirsten Heitland. 2010. "Seeing the Other Side: Reducing Political Partisanship via Self-Affirmation in the 2008 Presidential Election." *Analyses of Social Issues and Public Policy* 10 (1): 276–92.

Birnbaum, Jeffrey H., and Alan S. Murray. 1987. *Showdown at Gucci Gulch: Lawmakers, Lobbyists, and the Unlikely Triumph of Tax Reform.* New York: Vintage Books.

Bishin, Benjamin G. 2000. "Constituency Influence in Congress: Does Subconstituency Matter?" *Legislative Studies Quarterly* 25 (3): 389–415.

Boatright, Robert G. 2013. *Getting Primaried: The Changing Politics of Congressional Primary Challenges.* Ann Arbor: University of Michigan Press.

2014. *Congressional Primary Elections*. New York: Routledge.

Bolsen, Toby, James N. Druckman, and Fay Lomax Cook. 2014. "The Influence of Partisan Motivated Reasoning on Public Opinion." *Political Behavior* 36 (2): 235–62.

Bond, Jon R. 2013. "'Life Ain't Easy for a President Named Barack': Party, Ideology, and Tea Party Freshman Support for the Nation's First Black President." *The Forum* 11 (2): 243–58.

Bonica, Adam. 2013. "Ideology and Interests in the Political Marketplace." *American Journal of Political Science* 57 (2): 294–311.

Bornemeier, James. 1996. "Reform of Pesticide Rules Passes House Unanimously." *Los Angeles Times*, July 24, 1996. [cited September 5, 2017]. Available from http://articles.latimes.com/1996-07-24/news/mn-27420_1_agricultural-pesticides.

Bradner, Eric. 2015. "How secretive Is the Trans-Pacific Partnership?" *CNN*, June 12, 2015. [cited September 5, 2017]. Available from www.cnn.com/2015/06/11/politics/trade-deal-secrecy-tpp/index.html.

Brady, David W., Hahrie Han, and Jeremy C. Pope. 2007. "Primary Elections and Candidate Ideology: Out-of-Step with the Primary Electorate?" *Legislative Studies Quarterly* 32 (1): 79–105.

Brady, David W., and Craig Volden. 1998. *Revolving Gridlock*. Boulder: Westview Press.

Broockman, David E., and Daniel M. Butler. 2017. "The Causal Effects of Elite Position-Taking on Voter Attitudes: Field Experiments with Elite Communication." *American Journal of Political Science* 61 (1): 208–21.

Broockman, David E., and Christopher Skovron. 2018. "Bias in Perceptions of Public Opinion Among American Political Elites." *American Political Science Review* 112 (3): 542–63.

Brown, Bert R. 1977. "Face-Saving and Face-Restoration in Negotiation." In *Negotiations: Social-Psychological Perspectives*, ed. D. Druckman. Beverly Hills: Sage.

Bullock, Dennis R. 2016. "Of principle and compromise: A paradox within America's political discourse." *The Hill*, December 4, 2016. [cited January 26, 2018]. Available from http://thehill.com/blogs/congress-blog/politics/308578-of-principle-and-compromise-a-paradox-within-americas-political.

Burden, Barry C. 2001. "The Polarizing Effects of Congressional Primaries." In *Congressional Primaries and the Politics of Representation*, ed. P. F. Galderisi, M. Ezra, and M. Lyons. Lanham: Rowman & Littlefield. pp. 95–115.

2011. "Polarization, Obstruction, and Governing in the Senate." *The Forum* 9 (4):Article 4.

Butler, Daniel M. 2009. "The Effect of the Size of Voting Blocs on Incumbents' Roll-Call Voting and the Asymmetric Polarization of Congress." *Legislative Studies Quarterly* 34 (3): 297–318.

Butler, Daniel M., and Eleanor Neff Powell. 2014. "Understanding the Party Brand: Experimental Evidence on the Role of Valence." *The Journal of Politics* 76 (2): 492–505.

Butler, Daniel M., Craig Volden, Adam M. Dynes, and Boris Shor. 2017. "Ideology, Learning, and Policy Diffusion: Experimental Evidence." *American Journal of Political Science* 61 (1): 37–49.

Cameron, Charles M. 2000. *Veto Bargaining: Presidents and the Politics of Negative Power*. New York: Cambridge University Press.

Campbell, Angus, Phillip E. Converse, Warren E. Miller, and Donald E. Stokes. 1960. *The American Voter*. New York: Wiley.

Campbell, David E., and Robert D. Putnam. 2011. "Crashing the Tea Party." *The New York Times*, August 16, 2011. [cited August 18, 2017]. Available from www.nytimes.com/2011/08/17/opinion/crashing-the-tea-party.html?mcubz=0.

Canes-Wrone, Brandice, David W. Brady, and John F. Cogan. 2002. "Out of Step, Out of Office: Electoral Accountability and House Members' Voting." *American Political Science Review* 96 (1): 127–40.

Canes-Wrone, Brandice, William Minozzi, and Jessica Bonney Reveley. 2011. "Issue Accountability and the Mass Public." *Legislative Studies Quarterly* 36 (1): 5–35.

Cannon, Michael F. 2017. "GOP healthcare bill Is not repeal – it is ObamaCare-lite, or worse." *The Hill*, May 4, 2017. [cited February 4, 2019]. Available from https://thehill.com/blogs/pundits-blog/healthcare/331987-this-is-not-repeal-it-is-obamacare-lite-or-worse.

Carey, John M., Richard G. Niemi, Lynda W. Powell, and Gary Moncrief. 2002. *State Legislative Survey*. Ann Arbor, MI: Inter-university Consortium for Political and Social Research [distributor].

Carson, Jamie, Michael H. Crespin, Carrie P. Eaves, and Emily Wanless. 2011a. "Constituency Congruency and Candidate Competition in U.S. House Elections." *Legislative Studies Quarterly* 36 (3): 461–82.

Carson, Jamie, Michael H. Crespin, Carrie P. Eaves, and Emily O. Wanless. 2012. "Constituency Congruency and Candidate Competition in Primary Elections for the U.S. House." *State Politics & Policy Quarterly* 12 (2): 127–45.

Carson, Jamie L., Michael H. Crespin, Charles J. Finocchiaro, and David W. Rohde. 2007. "Redistricting and Party Polarization in the US House of Representatives." *American Politics Research* 35 (6): 878–904.

Carson, Jamie L., Gregory Koger, Matthew J. Lebo, and Everett Young. 2010. "The Electoral Costs of Party Loyalty in Congress." *American Journal of Political Science* 54 (3): 598–616.

Carson, Jamie L., Nathan W. Monroe, and Gregory Robinson. 2011b. "Unpacking Agenda Control in Congress: Individual Roll Rates and the Republican Revolution." *Political Research Quarterly* 64 (1): 17–30.

Chen, Min. 1993. "Tricks of the China Trade." *China Business Review* 20 (2): 12–16.

Claassen, Ryan L., and Stephen P. Nicholson. 2013. "Extreme Voices, Interest Groups and the Misrepresentation of Issue Publics." *Public Opinion Quarterly* 77 (4): 861–87.

Clifford, Scott, and Jennifer Jerit. 2013. "How Words Do the Work of Politics: Moral Foundations Theory and the Debate over Stem Cell Research." *The Journal of Politics* 75 (3): 659–71.

Clinton, Joshua D., and Adam Meirowitz. 2004. "Testing Explanations of Strategic Voting in Legislatures: A Reexamination of the Compromise of 1790." *American Journal of Political Science* 48 (4): 675–89.

CNN Political Unit. 2012. "In statement, Lugar defends campaign while criticizing partisan environment." *CNN Politics*, May 8, 2012. [cited April 20, 2018]. Available from http://politicalticker.blogs.cnn.com/2012/05/08/in-statement-lugar-defends-campaign-while-criticizing-partisan-environment/.

Cohen, Geoffrey L., David K. Sherman, Anthony Bastardi, Lillian Hsu, Michelle McGoey, and Lee Ross. 2007. "Bridging the Partisan Divide: Self-Affirmation Reduces Ideological Closed-Mindedness and Inflexibility in Negotiation." *Journal of Personality and Social Psychology* 93 (3): 415–30.

"Congressional Record, December 13." 2007. Washington, DC.

"Congressional Record, June 7." 2000. Washington, DC.

"Congressional Record, June 26." 2008. Washington, DC.

"Congressional Record, June 30." 2010. Washington, DC.

"Congressional Record, May 2." 1996. Washington, DC.

"Congressional Record, May 14." 2003. Washington, DC.

"Congressional Record, May 14." 2008. Washington, DC.

Converse, Phillip E. 1964. "The Nature of Belief Systems in Mass Publics." In *Ideology and Discontent*, ed. D. E. Apter. New York: Free Press. pp. 206–31.

Cox, Gary, and Mathew D. McCubbins. 1993. *Legislative Leviathan*. Berkeley: University of California Press.

2005. *Setting the Agenda: Responsible Party Government in the U.S. House of Representatives*. New York: Cambridge University Press.

Crisp, Brian F., Scott W. Desposato, and Kristin Kanthak. 2011. "Legislative Pivots, Presidential Powers, and Policy Stability." *The Journal of Law, Economics, and Organization* 27 (2): 426–52.

Curry, James M. 2015. *Legislating in the Dark: Information and Power in the House of Representatives*. Chicago: University of Chicago Press.

Curry, James M., and Frances E. Lee. 2016. "Congress is far more bipartisan than headlines suggest." *The Washington Post*. December 20, 2016. [cited March 10, 2017]. Available from www.washingtonpost.com/news/monkey-cage/wp/2016/12/20/congress-is-far-more-bipartisan-than-headlines-suggest/?utm_term=.314562d526c5.

Davey, Monica. 2012. "Lugar Loses Primary Challenge in Indiana." *The New York Times*, May 8, 2012. [cited April 20, 2018]. Available from www.nytimes.com/2012/05/09/us/politics/lugar-loses-primary-challenge-in-indiana.html.

DeBell, Matthew, Catherine Wilson, Gary Segura, Simon Jackman, and Vincent Hutchings. 2012. "Methodology Report and User's Guide for the ANES 2010–2012 Evaluations of Government and Society Study." ed. American National Election Study. Palo Alto, CA and Ann Arbor, MI: Stanford University and University of Michigan.

"Default Avoided at Eleventh Hour." 2011. In *CQ Almanac*, ed. J. Austin. Washington, DC: CQ-Roll Call Group, 2012.

Delli Carpini, Michael X., and Scott Keeter. 1996. *What Americans Know About Politics and Why It Matters*. New Haven: Yale University Press.

Demko, Paul. 2017. "How the Senate health bill became 'Obamacare lite'." *Politico*, July 6, 2017. [cited February 4, 2019]. Available from www.politico.com/story/2017/07/06/republican-senate-struggles-obamacare-240278.

Democratic Platform Committee. 2016. "2016 Democratic Party Platform." Available at www.presidency.ucsb.edu/documents/2016-democratic-party-platform.

Ditto, Peter H., and Andrew J. Mastronarde. 2009. "The Paradox of the Political Maverick." *Journal of Experimental Social Psychology* 45 (1): 295–98.

Downs, Anthony. 1957. *An Economic Theory of Democracy*. Boston: Addison-Wesley.

Druckman, Daniel. 1993. "The Situational Levers of Negotiating Flexibility." *Journal of Conflict Resolution* 37 (2): 236–76.

1994. "Determinants of Compromising Behavior in Negotiation: A Meta-Analysis." *Journal of Conflict Resolution* 38 (3): 507–56.

Druckman, Daniel. 1995. "Situational Levers of Position Change: Further Explorations." *The Annals of the American Academy of Political and Social Science* 542 (1): 61–80.

Druckman, Daniel, and James N. Druckman. 1996. "Visibility and Negotiating Flexibility." *The Journal of Social Psychology* 136 (1): 117–20.

Druckman, James N., Erik Peterson, and Rune Slothuus. 2013. "How Elite Partisan Polarization Affects Public Opinion Formation." *American Political Science Review* 107 (1): 57–79.

Durrant, Jeffrey O. 2007. *Struggle Over Utah's San Rafael Swell: Wilderness, National Conservation Areas, and National Monuments*. Tucson, AZ: The University of Arizona Press.

Egan, Patrick J. 2014. "'Do Something' Politics and Double-Peaked Policy Preferences." *Journal of Politics* 76 (2): 333–49.

Elving, Ronald D. 1995. *Conflict & Compromise: How Congress Makes the Law*. New York: Simon & Schuster.

Enelow, James M., and Melvin J. Hinich. 1984. *The Spatial Theory of Voting: An Introduction*. Cambridge: Cambridge University Press.

E&E Daily. 2010. "Senate Climate Debate: The 60-vote Climb." May 12, 2010. [cited March 22, 2018]. Available from www.eenews.net/eed/documents/climate_debate_senate.pdf.

Epstein, David, and Peter Zemsky. 1995. "Money Talks: Deterring Quality Challengers in Congressional Elections." *American Political Science Review* 89 (2): 295–308.

Esterling, Kevin M., Michael A. Neblo, and David M. J. Lazer. 2011. "Means, Motive, and Opportunity in Becoming Informed about Politics: A Deliberative Field Experiment with Members of Congress and Their Constituents." *Public Opinion Quarterly* 75 (3): 483–503.

Feinberg, Matthew, and Robb Willer. 2013. "The Moral Roots of Environmental Attitudes." *Psychological Science* 24 (1): 56–62.

Fenno, Richard F. Jr. 1978. *Home Style: Home Members in Their Districts*. Boston: Little, Brown.

Fiorina, Morris P. 1974. *Representatives, Roll Calls, and Constituencies.* Lexington, MA: Lexington Books.

1983. *Retrospective Voting in American National Elections.* New Haven: Yale University Press.

Fiorina, Morris P., Samuel Abrams, and Jeremy Pope. 2005. *Culture War? The Myth of a Polarized America.* New York: Pearson Longman.

Fisher, Samuel H. III, and Rebekah Herrick. 2013. "Old versus New: The Comparative Efficiency of Mail and Internet Surveys of State Legislators "*State Politics & Policy Quarterly* 13 (2): 147–63.

Flynn, D. J., and Laurel Harbridge. 2016. "How Partisan Conflict in Congress Affects Public Opinion: Strategies, Outcomes, and Issue Differences." *American Politics Research* 44 (5): 875–902.

Fowler, Linda L. 1982. "How Interest Groups Select Issues for Rating Voting Records of Members of the US Congress." *Legislative Studies Quarterly* 7 (3): 401–13.

Fox, Justin, and Lawrence Rothenberg. 2011. "Influence Without Bribes: A Noncontracting Model of Campaign Giving and Policymaking." *Political Analysis* 19 (3): 325–41.

Gaertner, Samuel L., and John F. Dovidio. 2011. "Common Ingroup Identity Model." In *The Encyclopedia of Peace Psychology*, ed. Daniel J. Christie. Malden: Blackwell Publishing Ltd.

Garcia, Monique, and Kim Geiger. 2017. "Madigan's House approves major income tax hike as Republicans break with Rauner." *Chicago Tribune*, July 2, 2017. [cited July 6, 2017]. Available from www.chicagotribune.com/news/local/politics/ct-illinois-budget-madigan-tax-hike-vote-met-0703-20170702-story.html.

Gerber, Elisabeth R., and Rebecca B. Morton. 1998. "Primary Election Systems and Representation." *Journal of Law, Economics, & Organization* 14 (2): 304–24.

Gilens, Martin. 2005. "Inequality and Democratic Responsiveness." *Public Opinion Quarterly* 69 (5): 778–96.

Gilens, Martin, and Benjamin I. Page. 2014. "Testing Theories of American Politics: Elites, Interest Groups, and Average Citizens." *Perspectives on Politics* 12 (3): 564–81.

Gilmour, John B. 1995. *Strategic Disagreement.* Pittsburgh: University of Pittsburgh Press.

Ginges, Jeremy, Scott Atran, Douglas Medin, and Khalil Shikaki. 2007. "Sacred Bounds on Rational Resolution of Violent Political Conflict." *Proceedings of the National Academy of Sciences* 104 (18): 7357–60.

Glaser, James M. 2006. "Public Support for Political Compromise on a Volatile Racial Issue: Insight from the Survey Experiment." *Political Psychology* 27 (3): 423–39.

Graham, Jesse, Jonathan Haidt, and Brian A. Nosek. 2009. "Liberals and Conservatives Rely on Different Sets of Moral Foundations." *Journal of Personality and Social Psychology* 96 (5): 1029.

Green, Donald, Bradley Palmquist, and Eric Schickler. 2002. *Partisan Hearts and Minds.* New Haven: Yale University Press.

Greene, Steven. 2004. "Social Identity Theory and Party Identification." *Social Science Quarterly* 85 (1): 136–53.

Griffin, John D., and Brian Newman. 2005. "Are Voters Better Represented?" *The Journal of Politics* 67 (4): 1206–27.

Grose, Christian R., Neil Malhotra, and Robert Parks Van Houweling. 2015. "Explaining Explanations: How Legislators Explain Their Policy Positions and How Citizens React." *American Journal of Political Science* 59 (3): 724–43.

Groseclose, Tim, and Nolan McCarty. 2001. "The Politics of Blame: Bargaining before an Audience." *American Journal of Political Science* 45 (1): 100–19.

Grossmann, Matt, and David A. Hopkins. 2015. "Ideological Republicans and Group Interest Democrats: The Asymmetry of American Party Politics." *Perspectives on Politics* 13 (1): 119–39.

Grumbach, Jacob M. 2018. "From Backwaters to Major Policymakers: Policy Polarization in the States, 1970–2014." *Perspectives on Politics* 16 (2): 416–35.

Grynaviski, Jeffrey D. 2010. *Partisan Bonds*. New York: Cambridge University Press.

Gutmann, Amy, and Dennis Thompson. 2012. *The Spirit of Compromise: Why Governing Demands It and Campaigning Undermines It*. Princeton: Princeton University Press.

Hall, Andrew B. 2015. "What Happens When Extremists Win Primaries?" *American Political Science Review* 109 (1): 18–42.

Hansen, John Mark. 1991. *Gaining Access: Congress and the Farm Lobby, 1919–1981*. Chicago: University of Chicago Press.

Harbridge, Laurel. 2015. *Is Bipartisanship Dead? Policy Agreement and Agenda-Setting in the House of Representatives*. New York: Cambridge University Press.

Harbridge, Laurel, and Neil Malhotra. 2011. "Electoral Incentives and Partisan Conflict in Congress: Evidence from Survey Experiments." *American Journal of Political Science* 55 (3): 1–17.

Harbridge, Laurel, Neil Malhotra, and Brian F. Harrison. 2014. "Public Preferences for Bipartisanship in the Policymaking Process." *Legislative Studies Quarterly* 39 (3): 327–55.

Harden, Jeffrey J. 2013. "Multidimensional Responsiveness: The Determinants of Legislators' Representational Priorities." *Legislative Studies Quarterly* 38 (2): 155–84.

Harden, Jeffrey J., and Justin H. Kirkland. 2016. "Do Campaign Donors Influence Polarization? Evidence from Public Financing in the American States." *Legislative Studies Quarterly* 41 (1): 119–52.

Hill, Seth J. 2015. "Institution of Nomination and the Policy Ideology of Primary Electorates." *Quarterly Journal of Political Science* 10 (4): 461–87.

Hirano, Shigeo, James M. Snyder, Stephen Daniel Ansolabehere, and John Mark Hansen. 2010. "Primary Elections and Partisan Polarization in the U.S. Congress." *Quarterly Journal of Political Science* 5 (2): 169–91.

Holbrook, Allyson L., Jon A. Krosnick, and Alison Pfent. 2008. "The Causes and Consequences of Response Rates in Surveys by the New Media and

Government Contractor Survey Research Firms." In *Advances in Telephone Survey Methodology*, ed. J. M. Lepkowski, C. Tucker, J. M. Brick, E. de Lecuw, L. Japec, P. J. Lavrakas, M. W. Link, and R. L. Sangster. Hoboken: John Wiley & Sons. pp. 499–528.

House of Representatives Resources Committee. 2000. "Report on the San Rafael Western Legacy District and National Conservation Act to Accompany H.R. 3605." Washington, DC.

Hujer, Marc, and Gregor Peter Schmitz. 2011. "Interview with Tea Party Co-Founder Mark Meckler 'We Have Compromised Our Way Into Disaster'." *Spiegel Online*, August 1, 2011. [cited April 10, 2018]. Available from www.spiegel.de/international/world/interview-with-tea-party-co-founder-mark-meckler-we-have-compromised-our-way-into-disaster-a-777705.html.

Humphreys, Macartan, Raul Sanchez de la Sierra, and Peter van der Windt. 2013. "Fishing, Commitment, and Communication: A Proposal for Comprehensive Nonbinding Research Registration." *Political Analysis* 21 (1): 1–20.

Huntsman, Jon, and Joe Manchin, eds. 2014. *No Labels: A Shared Vision for a Stronger America*. New York: Diversion Books.

Hutchings, Vincent, Ted Brader, Shanto Iyengar, Gary Segura, and Simon Jackman. 2017. "User's Guide and Codebook for the ANES 2016 Time Series Study." ed. American National Election Study. Palo Alto and Ann Arbor: Stanford University and University of Michigan.

  2018. "American National Election Studies Time Series Cumulative Data File 1948–2016." ed. American National Election Study. Palo Alto and Ann Arbor: Stanford University and University of Michigan.

Inskeep, Steve. 2019. "We Need to Work Together to Reopen Government, Rep. Suozzi Says." *NPR Morning Edition*, January 17, 2019. [cited February 1, 2019]. Available from www.npr.org/2019/01/17/686135349/we-need-to-work-together-to-reopen-government-rep-suozzi-says.

Interview with Ronald Reagan. 1980. "An Extremist? 'I'll Run on My Record'." *U.S. News & World Report*, May 5, 1980, Retrieved from Nexis Uni.

Iyengar, Shanto, Kyu S. Hahn, Jon A. Krosnick, and John Walker. 2008. "Selective Exposure to Campaign Communication: The Role of Anticipated Agreement and Issue Public Membership." *The Journal of Politics* 70 (1): 186–200.

Jacobson, Gary C. 2011. "The President, the Tea Party, and Voting Behavior in 2010: Insights from the Cooperative Congressional Election Study." Paper presented at the *Annual Meeting of the American Political Science Association*. Seattle.

  2014. "Strategic Politicians and the Dynamics of U.S. House Elections, 1946–86." *American Political Science Review* 83 (3): 773–93.

Jacobson, Gary C., and Samuel Kernell. 1983. *Strategy and Choice in Congressional Elections*. 2nd ed. New Haven: Yale University Press.

Janofsky, Michael. 2000. "Tire Tracks Ignite a Debate About Pristine Tract in Utah." *The New York Times*, March 11, 2000. [cited January 26, 2019]. Available from www.nytimes.com/2000/03/11/us/tire-tracks-ignite-a-debate-about-pristine-tract-in-utah.html.

Jansa, Joshua M., and Michele M. Hoyman. 2018. "Do Unions Punish Democrats? Free-Trade Votes and Labor PAC Contributions, 1999–2012." *Political Research Quarterly* 71 (2): 424–39.

Jessee, Stephen A. 2009. "Spatial Voting in the 2004 Presidential Election." *American Political Science Review* 103 (1): 59–81.

  2012. *Ideology and Spatial Voting in American Elections.* New York: Cambridge University Press.

Jochim, Ashley E., and Bryan D. Jones. 2013. "Issue Politics in a Polarized Congress." *Political Research Quarterly* 66 (2): 352–69.

Joesten, Danielle A., and Walter J. Stone. 2014. "Reassessing Proximity Voting: Expertise, Party, and Choice in Congressional Elections." *The Journal of Politics* 76 (3): 740–53.

Jones, Bryan D., Tracy Sulkin, and Heather R. Larsen. 2003. "Policy Punctuations in American Political Institutions." *American Political Science Review* 97 (1): 151–69.

Jordan, Karen, and Cheryl Burton. 2018. "Des Plaines adopts vaping ordinance supported by Main West High School." *ABC 7 News*, May 7, 2018. [cited January 22, 2019]. Available from https://abc7chicago.com/health/des-plaines-adopts-vaping-ordinance-supported-by-maine-west/3440337/.

Kahan, Dan M., and Donald Braman. 2006. "Cultural Cognition and Public Policy." *Yale Law & Policy Review* 24 (1): 149–72.

Kalla, Joshua L., and David E. Broockman. 2017. "The Minimal Persuasive Effects of Campaign Contact in General Elections: Evidence from 49 Field Experiments." *American Political Science Review* 112 (1): 148–66.

Kanthak, Kristin. 2002. "Top-Down Divergence: The Effect of Party-Determined Power on Candidate Ideological Placement." *Journal of Theoretical Politics* 14 (3): 301–23.

Kanthak, Kristin, and Rebecca Morton. 2001. "The Effects of Electoral Rules on Congressional Primaries." In *Congressional Primaries and the Politics of Representation,* ed. P.F. Galderisi, M. Ezra, and M. Lyons. Boulder: Rowman & Littlefield Publishers. pp. 116–31.

Karol, David. 2015. "Party Activists, Interest Groups, and Polarization in American Politics." In *American Gridlock: The Sources, Character, and Impact of Political Polarization,* ed. J. A. Thurber and A. Yoshinaka. New York: Cambridge University Press. pp. 68–85.

Karpowitz, Christopher F., and Jane Mansbridge. 2005. "Disagreement and Consensus: The Importance of Dynamic Updating in Public Deliberation." In *The Deliberative Democracy Handbook,* ed. J. Gastil and P. Levine. San Francisco: Jossey-Bass. pp. 237–53.

Karpowitz, Christopher F., and Tali Mendelberg. 2007. "Groups and Deliberation." *Swiss Political Science Review* 13 (4): 645–62.

Karpowitz, Christopher F., Tali Mendelberg, and L. E. E. Shaker. 2012. "Gender Inequality in Deliberative Participation." *American Political Science Review* 106 (3): 533–47.

Karpowitz, Christopher F., J. Quin Monson, Kelly D. Patterson, and Jeremy C. Pope. 2011. "Tea Time in America? The Impact of the Tea Party Movement on the 2010 Midterm Elections." *PS: Political Science & Politics* 44 (2): 303–9.

Key, Valdimer O. 1949. *Southern Politics in State and Nation*. New York: Knopf.

Key, Vladimir O. 1966. *The Responsible Electorate: Rationality in Presidential Voting, 1936–1960*. Cambridge: Belknap Press of Harvard University Press.

Kinder, Donald R., and Nathan P. Kalmoe. 2017. *Neither Liberal nor Conservative: Ideological Innocence in the American Public*. Chicago: University of Chicago Press.

Kingdon, John W. 1973. *Congressmen's Voting Decisions*. New York: Harper and Row.

Kirkland, Justin H., and Jeffrey J. Harden. 2016. "Representation, Competing Principals, and Waffling on Bills in US Legislatures." *Legislative Studies Quarterly* 41 (3): 657–86.

Klar, Samara. 2013. "The Influence of Competing Identity Primes on Political Preferences." *The Journal of Politics* 75 (4): 1108–24.

Koger, Gregory. 2003. "Position Taking and Cosponsorship in the U.S. House." *Legislative Studies Quarterly* 28 (2): 225–46.

Koger, Gregory, and Matthew J. Lebo. 2017. *Strategic Party Government: Why Winning Trumps Ideology*. Chicago: University of Chicago Press.

Korecki, Natasha. 2017. "Illinois lawmakers face budget rage." *Politico*, July 5, 2017. [cited July 6, 2017]. Available from www.politico.com/story/2017/07/05/illinois-budget-rage-240243.

Kousser, Thad, and Justin H. Phillips. 2009. "Who Blinks First? Legislative Patience and Bargaining with Governors." *Legislative Studies Quarterly* 34 (1): 55–86.

Kramer, Roderick M., Pamela Pommerenke, and Elizabeth Newton. 1993. "The Social Context of Negotiation: Effects of Social Identity and Interpersonal Accountability on Negotiator Decision Making." *Journal of Conflict Resolution* 37 (4): 633–54.

Krehbiel, Keith. 1998. *Pivotal Politics*. Chicago: University of Chicago Press.

Krehbiel, Keith, and Douglas Rivers. 1988. "The Analysis of Committee Power: An Application to Senate Voting on the Minimum Wage." *American Journal of Political Science* 32 (4): 1151–74.

Krosnick, Jon A. 1990. "Government Policy and Citizen Passion: A Study of Issue Publics in Contemporary America." *Political Behavior* 12 (1): 59–92.

Krosnick, Jon A., Matthew K. Berent, and David S. Boninger. 1994. "Pockets of Responsibility in the American Electorate: Findings of a Research Program on Attitude Importance." *Political Communication* 11 (4): 391–411.

Krosnick, Jon, and Shibley Telhami. 1995. "Public Attitudes Toward Israel: A Study of the Attentive and Issue Publics." *International Studies Quarterly* 39 (4): 535–44.

Kull, Steven, and I. M. Destler. 1999. *Misreading the Public: The Myth of a New Isolationism*. Washington, DC: Brooking Institution Press.

Kuster, Ann McLane. 2013. "Kuster Calls for Common Sense, Compromise In Speech at New England Council." May 11, 2013. House of Representatives, Member Press Release. [cited March 22, 2018]. Available from https://kuster.house.gov/media-center/press-releases/kuster-calls-for-common-sense-compromise-in-speech-at-new-england.

La Raja, Raymond J., and Brian F. Schaffner. 2015. *Campaign Finance and Political Polarization: When Purists Prevail*. Ann Arbor: University of Michigan Press.

Lakoff, George. 2002. *Moral Politics: How Liberals and Conservatives Think*. 2nd ed. Chicago: University of Chicago Press.

2014. *The All New Don't Think of an Elephant!: Know Your Values and Frame the Debate*. White River Junction: Chelsea Green Publishing.

Lane, Eric, and Michael Oreskes. 2007. *The Genius of America: How the Constitution Saved Our Country – and Why It Can Again*. New York: Bloomsbury Press.

Lavine, Howard, Christopher Johnston, and Marco Steenbergen. 2012. *The Ambivalent Partisan*. New York: Oxford University Press.

Lebo, Matthew J., Adam J. McGlynn, and Gregory Koger. 2007. "Strategic Party Government: Party Influence in Congress, 1789–2000." *American Journal of Political Science* 51 (3): 464–81.

Lee, Frances E. 2009. *Beyond Ideology: Politics, Principles, and Partisanship in the U.S. Senate*. Chicago: University of Chicago Press.

2016. *Insecure Majorities: Congress and the Perpetual Campaign*. Chicago: University of Chicago Press.

Leighley, Jan E., and Jennifer Oser. 2017. "Representation in an Era of Political and Economic Inequality: How and When Citizen Engagement Matters." *Perspectives on Politics* 16 (2): 328–44.

Lenz, Gabriel S. 2013. *Follow the Leader? How Voters Response to Politicians' Policies and Performance*. Chicago: University of Chicago Press.

Lerner, Jennifer S., and Philip E. Tetlock. 1999. "Accounting for the Effects of Accountability." *Psychological Bulletin* 125 (2): 255–75.

Levendusky, Matthew. 2009. *The Partisan Sort: How Liberals Became Democrats and Conservatives Became Republicans*. Chicago: University of Chicago Press.

Levitt, Stephen. 1996. "How Do Senators Vote? Disentangling the Role of Voter Preferences, Party Affiliation, and Senator Ideology." *American Economic Review* 86 (2): 425–41.

Lin, C.-Y. Cynthia, and Lea Prince. 2009. "The Optimal Gas Tax for California." *Energy Policy* 37 (12): 5173–83.

Lott, Trent, and Tom Daschle. 2017. *Crisis Point: Why We Must – and How We Can – Overcome Our Broken Politics in Washington and Across America*. New York: Bloomsbury Press.

Maestas, Cherie, Grant W. Neeley, and Jr. Lilliard E. Richardson. 2003. "The State of Surveying Legislators: Dilemmas and Suggestions." *State Politics & Policy Quarterly* 3 (1): 90–108.

Mann, Thomas, and Norman J. Ornstein. 2012. *It's Even Worse Than It Looks: How the American Constitutional System Collided with the Politics of Extremism*. New York: Basic Books.

Maoz, Ifat. 2012. "Threats versus Promises: How the Framing of Concession Appeals in News Coverage Affects Support for Compromise." *International Journal of Communication* 6: 2280–300.

Mason, George. 1892. "Letter to His Son on May 27, 1787." In *The Life of George Mason, 1725–1792*, ed. K. M. Rowland. New York: G.P. Putnam's Sons.

Mason, Lilliana. 2013. "The Rise of Uncivil Agreement: Issue versus Behavioral Polarization in the American Electorate." *American Behavioral Scientist* 57 (1): 140–59.

2015. "'I Disrespectfully Agree': The Differential Effects of Partisan Sorting on Social and Issue Polarization." *American Journal of Political Science* 59 (1): 128–45.

Mayhew, David R. 1974. *Congress: The Electoral Connection*. New Haven: Yale University Press.

1991. *Divided We Govern*. New Haven: Yale University Press.

McCarty, Nolan, Keith T. Poole, and Howard Rosenthal. 2006. *Polarized America: The Dance of Ideology and Unequal Riches*. Cambridge: Massachusetts Institute of Technology Press.

McCormack, John. 2011. "Toomey: Dems Rejected Compromise, Demanded $1 Trillion Tax Hike." *The Weekly Standard*, November 22, 2011. [cited July 19, 2017]. Available from www.weeklystandard.com/toomey-dems-rejected-compromise-demanded-1-trillion-tax-hike/article/610027.

McGhee, Eric, Seth Masket, Boris Shor, Steven Rogers, and Nolan McCarty. 2014. "A Primary Cause of Partisanship? Nomination Systems and Legislator Ideology." *American Journal of Political Science* 58 (2): 337–51.

McGhee, Eric, and Boris Shor. 2017. "Has the Top Two Primary Elected More Moderates?" *Perspectives on Politics* 15 (4): 1053–66.

McGreevy, Patrick. 2017. "He rallied support for California's climate change fight. Now Chad Mayes is out as Assembly Republican leader." *Los Angeles Times*, August 24, 2017. [cited February 4, 2018]. Available from www.latimes.com/politics/la-pol-ca-republicans-assembly-leader-dahle-20170824-story.html.

Memoli, Michael A. 2014. "Eric Cantor upset: How Dave Brat pulled off a historic Political Coup." *Los Angeles Times*, June 11, 2014. [cited August 18, 2017]. Available from www.latimes.com/nation/politics/politicsnow/la-pn-eric-cantor-dave-brat-primary-20140611-story.html.

Miller, Warren R., and Donald E. Stokes. 1963. "Constituency Influence in Congress." *American Political Science Review* 57 (1): 45–56.

Moe, Alexandra. 2010. "Just 32% of Tea Party Candidates Win." *NBC News*, November 3, 2010. [cited August 18, 2017]. Available from http://firstread.nbcnews.com/_news/2010/11/03/5403120-just-32-of-tea-party-candidates-win.

Monogan, James E. III 2013. "A Case for Registering Studies of Political Outcomes: An Application in the 2010 House Elections." *Political Analysis* 21 (1): 21–37.

Montanaro, Domenico. 2018. "John McCain Makes an Appeal for Civility and Humility." *NPR*, May 1, 2018. [cited May 2, 2018]. Available from www.npr.org/2018/05/01/607193169/john-mccain-makes-an-appeal-for-civility-and-humility.

Montgomery, Jacob M., Brendan Nyhan, and Michelle Torres. 2018. "How Conditioning on Posttreatment Variables Can Ruin Your Experiment and What to Do about It." *American Journal of Political Science* 62 (3): 760–75.

Mooney, Christopher Z., and Richard G. Schuldt. 2008. "Does Morality Policy Exist? Testing a Basic Assumption." *Policy Studies Journal* 36 (2): 199–218.

Nall, Clayton. 2015. "The Political Consequences of Spatial Policies: How Interstate Highways Facilitated Geographic Polarization." *The Journal of Politics* 77 (2): 394–406.

National Conference of State Legislatures. 2013. *Women in State Legislatures: 2013 Legislative Session.* [cited July 21, 2014]. Available from www.ncsl.org/legislators-sta/legislators/womens-legislative-network/women-in-state-legislatures-for-2013.aspx.

2014. *NCSL 'Transportation Funding and Finance Legislation Database.* [cited April 23, 2018]. Available from www.ncsl.org/research/transportation/ncsl-transportation-funding-nance-legis-database.aspx.

Neblo, Michael A., Kevin M. Esterling, Ryan P. Kennedy, David M. J. Lazer, and Anand E. Sokhey. 2010. "Who Wants to Deliberate—And Why?" *American Political Science Review* 104 (3): 566–83.

Newport, Frank. 2017. "Americans Favor Compromise to Get Things Done in Washington." *Gallup*, October 9, 2017. [cited January 26, 2018]. Available from http://news.gallup.com/poll/220265/americans-favor-compromise-things-done-washington.aspx?g_source=POLITICS&g_medium=topic&g_campaign=tiles.

Newport, Frank, and Lydia Saad. 2016. "Congress' Harshest Critics Identify a Crisis of Influence." *Gallup.* [cited August 2, 2016]. Available from www.gallup.com/poll/193079/congress-harshest-critics-identify-crisis-influence.aspx.

No Labels. 2016. *No Labels Stakes Out a National Agenda*, February 2, 2016. [cited July 17, 2017]. Available from www.nolabels.org/blog/press/no-labels-stakes-out-a-national-agenda/.

2017. *No Labels Philosophy.* [cited July 19, 2017]. Available from www.nolabels.org/philosophy/.

Norrander, Barbara, and Jay Wendland. 2016. "Open versus Closed Primaries and the Ideological Composition of Presidential Primary Electorates." *Electoral Studies* 42: 229–36.

North, Douglass C. 1990. *Institutions, Institutional Change and Economic Performance.* New York: Cambridge University Press.

Nyhan, Brendan, Eric McGhee, John Sides, Seth Masket, and Steven Greene. 2012. "One Vote Out of Step? The Effects of Salient Roll Call Votes in the 2010 Election." *American Politics Research* 40 (5): 844–79.

Olivella, Santiago, Kristin Kanthak, and Brian F. Crisp. 2017. "…And Keeping Your Enemies Closer: Building Reputations for Facing Electoral Challenges." *Electoral Studies* 46: 75–86.

Paletta, Damian, and Jeff Stein. 2017. "Sweeping Tax Overhaul Clears Congress." *The Washington Post*, December 20, 2017. [cited February 4, 2019]. Available from www.washingtonpost.com/business/economy/gop-tax-bill-passes-congress-as-trump-prepares-to-sign-it-into-law/2017/12/20/0ba2fd98-e597-11e7-9ec2-518810e7d44d_story.html?utm_term=.3290572894ab.

Paris, Celia. 2017. "Breaking Down Bipartisanship: When and Why Citizens React to Cooperation Across Party Lines." *Public Opinion Quarterly* 81 (2): 473–94.

Parker, Christopher S., and Matt A. Barreto. 2014. *Change They Can't Believe In: The Tea Party and Reactionary Politics in America-Updated Edition.* Princeton: Princeton University Press.

Parry, Ian W. H., and Kenneth A. Small. 2005. "Does Britain or the United States Have the Right Gasoline Tax?" *The American Economic Review* 95 (4): 1276–89.

Patty, John W. 2016. "Signaling Through Obstruction." *American Journal of Political Science* 60 (1): 175–89.

Pear, Robert, and Thomas Kaplan. 2017. "House Republicans Unveil Plan to Replace Health Laq." *The New York Times*, March 6, 2017.

Pearson, Rick. 2018. "House Republican Leader Jim Durkin Faces Rare Primary Challenge, Symbolizing GOP Conflict." *Chicago Tribune*, March 16, 2018. [cited March 27, 2018]. Available from www.chicagotribune.com/news/local/politics/ct-met-jim-durkin-primary-challenge-20180316-story.html.

Pendergast, William R. 1990. "Managing the Negotiation Agenda." *Negotiation Journal* 6 (2): 135–45.

Penn, Elizabeth Maggie. 2009. "A Model of Farsighted Voting." *American Journal of Political Science* 53 (1): 36–54.

Perkins, Luke. 2017. "Attempt to Spare Hospitals a $264 Million Cut in Limbo." *The Durango Herald*, May 1, 2017. [cited July 17, 2017]. Available from https://durangoherald.com/articles/154945-state-democrats-reject-compromise-on-hospital-fee.

Petty, Richard E., and John T. Cacioppo. 1984. "Source Factors and the Elaboration Likelihood Model of Persuasion." *ACR North American Advances.*

Petty, Richard E., and John T. Cacioppo. 1986. "The Elaboration Likelihood Model of Persuasion." *Advances in Experimental Social Psychology* 19: 123–205.

Pew. 2011. *Most Want Budget Compromise but Split on Who's to Blame for Shutdown.* Pew Research Center Publications, April 4, 2011. [cited September 21, 2017]. Available from www.pewresearch.org/2011/04/04/most-want-budget-compromise-but-split-on-whos-to-blame-for-a-shutdown/.

———. 2012. *Trends in American Values: 1987–2012.* The Pew Research Center for People and the Press 2012. [cited July 9, 2012]. Available from www.people-press.org/files/legacy-pdf/06-04-12%20Values%20Release.pdf.

———. 2013. *Anger at Government Most Pronounced among Conservative Republicans* [Report]. Pew Research Center, September 20, 2013. [cited January 26, 2018]. Available from www.people-press.org/2013/09/30/anger-at-government-most-pronounced-among-conservative-republicans/.

———. 2014a. "2014 Political Polarization and Typology Survey." Pew Research Center. [cited April 20, 2018]. Available from www.people-press.org/2014/06/12/political-polarization-in-the-american-public/.

———. 2014b. *Beyond Red vs. Blue: The Political Typology.* Pew Research Center, June 26, 2014. [cited September 21, 2017]. Available from www.people-press.org/2014/06/26/the-political-typology-beyond-red-vs-blue/.

Poole, Keith T., and Howard Rosenthal. 1997. *Congress: A Political-Economic History of Roll Call Voting.* New York: Oxford University Press.

Rabinowitz, George, and Stuart Elaine Macdonald. 2014. "A Directional Theory of Issue Voting." *American Political Science Review* 83 (1): 93–121.

Ragusa, Jordan M., and Anthony Gaspar. 2016. "Where's the Tea Party? An Examination of the Tea Party's Voting Behavior in the House of Representatives." *Political Research Quarterly* 69 (2): 361–72.

Ramey, Adam. 2015. "Weighing the Alternatives: Preferences, Parties, and Constituency in Roll-Call Voting." *The Journal of Politics* 77 (2): 421–32.

Rand, A. Barry. 2013. "The Road Forward: Social Security and Medicare" [Blog]. *The Huffington Post*, January 20, 2013. [cited July 27, 2016]. Available from www.huffingtonpost.com/a-barry-rand/social-security-medicare_b_2513928.html.

Reid, Harry. 2012. "DNC 2012: Senator Harry Reid's Speech to the Democratic Convention." *The Washington Post*, September 4, 2012. [cited August 24, 2016]. Available from www.washingtonpost.com/politics/dnc-2012-senator-harry-reids-speech-to-democratic-convention-full-speech/2012/09/04/69571634-f6f2-11e1-8253-3f495ae70650_story.html?utm_term=.ea5e8bf6f7b4.

Republican Platform Committee. 2016. "Republican Party Platform 2016." Available at www.presidency.ucsb.edu/documents/2016-republican-party-platform.

Richard, Brandon. 2018. "Terri Bryant Defeats GOP Primary Challenger." *WSIL ABC*, March 20, 2018. [cited March 27, 2018]. Available from www.wsiltv.com/story/37772301/terri-bryant-defeats-gop-primary-challenger.

Rigby, Elizabeth, and Gerald C. Wright. 2015. "The Policy Consequences of Party Polarization: Evidence from the American States." In *American Gridlock: The Sources, Character, and Impact of Partisan Polarization*, ed. J. A. Thurber and A. Yoshinaka. New York: Cambridge University Press. pp. 236–55.

Ritov, Ilana, and Jonathan Baron. 1999. "Protected Values and Omission Bias." *Organizational Behavior and Human Decision Processes* 79 (2): 79–94.

Rojas, Alexandra, and Sean Mcelwee. 2019. "A Democrats Who Votes with Trump 69% of the Time Should Be Primaried." *CNN*, January 15, 2019. [cited January 25, 2019]. Available from www.cnn.com/2019/01/14/opinions/importance-of-challenging-democratic-incumbents-rojas-mcelwee/index.html.

Rosenbaum, David E. 1986. "The Tax Reform Act of 1986: How the Measure Came Together." *The New York Times*, October 23, 1986. [cited April 13, 2018]. Available from www.nytimes.com/1986/10/23/business/tax-reform-act--measure-came-together-tax-bill-for-textbooks.html?pagewanted=all.

Rosenbluth, Frances McCall, and Ian Shapiro. 2018. *Responsible Parties: Saving Democratic from Itself.* New Haven: Yale University Press.

Rosenthal, Alan. 2009. *Engines of Democracy: Politics and Policymaking in State Legislatures.* Washington, DC: CQ Press.

Ryan, Timothy J. 2014. "Reconsidering Moral Issues in Politics." *The Journal of Politics* 76 (2): 380–97.

2017. "No Compromise: Political Consequences of Moralized Attitudes." *American Journal of Political Science* 61 (2): 409–23.

Sacramento Bee Editorial Board. 2017. "Here's Why to Support Jerry Brown's Cap and Trade Deal." *The Sacramento Bee*, July 17, 2017. [cited January 26, 2018]. Available from www.sacbee.com/opinion/editorials/article160849844.html.

Samuelson, Robert J. 2013. "Ideology Is What Has Won in the Shutdown Debate." *The Washington Post*, October 6, 2013. [cited June 3, 2014]. Available from www.washingtonpost.com/opinions/robert-samuelson-the-shutdown-is-a-triumph-of-ideology/2013/10/06/1bc17054-2d4c-11e3-97a3-ff2758228523_story.html.

Sanchez, Raf. 2014. "Tea Party Victory Dashes Barack Obama's Lingering Hopes for a Compromise with Republicans." *The Telegraph*, June 11, 2014. [cited December 7, 2015]. Available from www.telegraph.co.uk/news/worldnews/republicans/10893084/Tea-Party-victory-dashes-Barack-Obamas-lingering-hopes-for-compromise-with-Republicans.html.

Sax, Linda J., Shannon K. Gilmartin, and Alyssa N. Bryant. 2003. "Assessing Response Rates and Nonresponse Bias in Web and Paper Surveys." *Research in Higher Education* 44 (4): 409–32.

Schaffner, Brian, and Stephen Ansolabehere. 2015. "CCES Common Content, 2014." Harvard Dataverse, V4, UNF:6:WvvlTX+E+iNraxwbaWNVdg== [fileUNF].

Schaper, David. 2014. *GOP Leaders: Gas Tax Hike Could Fuel Fixes to Bad Roads and Bridges*. NPR.org, December 8, 2014. [cited October 12, 2016]. Available from www.npr.org/2014/12/08/369373660/gop-leaders-gas-tax-hike-could-fuel-fixes-to-bad-roads-and-bridges.

Schwartz, Shalom H. 1977. "Normative Influences on Altruism." *Advances in Experimental Social Psychology* 10: 221–79.

1992. "Universals in the Content and Structure of Values: Theoretical Advances and Empirical Tests in 20 Countries." *Advances in Experimental Social Psychology* 21: 1–65.

Sernoffsky, Evan. 2017. "Protestors Shut Down Pelosi News Conference in DACA: 'All of Us or None of Us'." *San Francisco Chronicle*, September 18, 2017. [cited October 25, 2017]. Available from www.sfchronicle.com/news/article/Protesters-shut-down-Pelosi-news-conference-on-12206788.php.

Serrano, Jose. 2016. "The Serrano Report." In *Congressman Serrano Votes in Support of PROMESA*. Washington, DC: House of Representatives Member Newsletter.

Shapiro, Catherine R., David W. Brady, Richard A. Brody, and John A. Ferejohn. 1990. "Linking Constituency Opinion and Senate Voting Scores: A Hybrid Explanation." *Legislative Studies Quarterly* 15 (4): 599–621.

Sherman, Jake. 2014. "Cantor Loses." *Politico*, June 11, 2014. [cited October 12, 2016]. Available from www.politico.com/story/2014/06/eric-cantor-primary-election-results-virginia-107683.

Shor, Boris, and Nolan McCarty. 2011. "The Ideological Mapping of American Legislatures." *American Political Science Review* 104 (3): 530–51.

Siders, David, and Carla Marinucci. 2018. "California Democrats Decline to Endorse Feinstein." *Politico*, February 25, 2018. [cited March 26, 2018]. Available from www.sfgate.com/politics/article/Feinstein-answers-questions-still-gets-hard-10957888.php.

Sides, John, Chris Tausanovitch, Lynn Vavreck, and Christopher Warshaw. 2018. "On the Representativeness of Primary Electorates." *British Journal of Political Science*: 1–9 doi:10.1017/S000712341700062X.

Skocpol, Theda, and Vanessa Williamson. 2012. *The Tea Party and the Remaking of Republican Conservatism*. New York: Oxford University Press.

Skovron, Christopher. 2018. "What Politicians Believe About Electoral Accountability." SSRN. [cited January 8, 2019]. Available from https://papers.ssrn.com/sol3/papers.cfm?abstract_id=3309906.

Snyder, James M. 1992. "Artificial Extremism in Interest Group Ratings." *Legislative Studies Quarterly* 17 (3): 319–45.

Solomon, Christopher. 2016. *The Massive Land Deal That Could Change the West Forever*. Outside Online, February 22, 2016. [cited March 18, 2019]. Available from www.outsideonline.com/2056806/devils-grand-bargain-rob-bishop-western-lands.

Spetalnick, Matt. 2015. "Obama Defends TPP Secrecy, Says Now Is Chance for Debate." November 20, 2015. [cited September 5, 2017]. Available from www.reuters.com/article/us-trade-tpp-usa/obama-defends-tpp-secrecy-says-now-is-chance-for-debate-idUSKCN0T91GQ20151120.

Spielvogel, Christian. 2005. "'You Know Where I Stand': Moral Framing of the War on Terrorism and the Iraq War in the 2004 Presidential Campaign." *Rhetoric & Public Affairs* 8 (4): 549–69.

Squire, Peverill. 2007. "Measuring State Legislative Professionalism: The Squire Index Revisited." *State Politics & Policy Quarterly* 7 (2): 211–27.

Squire, Peverill, and Gary Moncrief. 2015. *State Legislatures Today: Politics Under the Domes*. Lanham: Rowman and Littlefield.

Stasavage, David. 2007. "Polarization and Publicity: Rethinking the Benefits of Deliberative Democracy." *The Journal of Politics* 69 (1): 59–72.

Stone, Walter J., and Elizabeth N. Simas. 2010. "Candidate Valence and Ideological Positions in U.S. House Elections." *American Journal of Political Science* 52 (2): 371–88.

Tamu, Jordan. 2011. "In Defense of the Back-Room Deal." *The New York Times*, October 18, 2011. [cited January 4, 2018]. Available from www.nytimes.com/2011/10/19/opinion/secrecy-helps-committees-negotiate.html.

Tausanovitch, Chris, and Christopher Warshaw. 2013. "Measuring Constituent Policy Preferences in Congress, State Legislatures, and Cities." *The Journal of Politics* 75 (2): 330–42.

Taylor, Shelley E., and Lien B. Pham. 1999. "The Effect of Mental Simulation on Goal-Directed Performance." *Imagination, Cognition and Personality* 18 (4): 253–68.

Taylor, Shelley E., Lien B. Pham, Inna D. Rivkin, and David A. Armor. 1998. "Harnessing the Imagination: Mental Simulation, Self-Regulation, and Coping." *American Psychologist* 53 (4): 429–39.

Tetlock, Philip E. 1983. "Accountability and Complexity of Thought." *Journal of Personality and Social Psychology* 45 (1): 74–83.

Theriault, Sean M. 2008. *Party Polarization in Congress*. New York: Cambridge University Press.

2015. "The Ugly Side of Party Polarization in Congress." In *American Gridlock: The Sources, Character, and Impact of Political Polarization*, ed. J. A. Thurber and A. Yoshinaka. New York: Cambridge University Press. pp. 152–70.

Thomsen, Danielle M. 2017. *Opting Out of Congress: Partisan Polarization.* New York: Cambridge University Press.

Trounstine, Jessica. 2009. "All Politics Is Local: The Reemergence of the Study of City Politics." *Perspectives on Politics* 7 (3): 611–18.

Tsebelis, George. 2002. *Veto Players: How Political Institutions Work.* Princeton: Princeton University Press.

Vinicky, Amanda. 2017. "State Rep. Steven Andersson to Step Down." *WTTW: Chicago Tonight*, August 17, 2017. [cited February 4, 2018]. Available from http://chicagotonight.wttw.com/2017/08/17/state-rep-steven-andersson-step-down.

Vogel, Kennth P., and Ben Smith. 2011. "Kochs' Plan for 2012: Raise $88M." *Politico*, February 11, 2012. [cited March 25, 2019]. Available from www.politico.com/story/2011/02/kochs-plan-for-2012-raise-88m-049303.

Volden, Craig. 1998. "Sophisticated Voting in Supermajoritarian Settings." *The Journal of Politics* 60 (1): 149–73.

Volden, Craig, and Alan E. Wiseman. 2007. "Bargaining in Legislatures over Particularistic and Collective Goods." *American Political Science Review* 101 (1): 79–92.

2014. *The Lawmakers: Legislative Effectiveness in the United States Congress.* New York: Cambridge University Press.

Walton, Richard E., and Robert B. McKersie. 1965. *A Behavioral Theory of Labor Negotiations: An Analysis of a Social Interaction System.* New York: McGraw-Hill.

Warren, Mark E., Jane Mansbridge, and Max A. Cameron with André Bächtiger, Simone Chambers, John Ferejohn, Alan Jacobs, Jack Knight, Daniel Naurin, Melissa Schwartzberg, Yael Tamir, Dennis Thompson, and Melissa Williams. 2016. "Deliberative Negotiation." In *Political Negotiation: A Handbook*, ed. J. Mansbridge and C. J. Martin. Washington, DC: Brookings. pp. 141–96.

Washington Post Editorial Board. 2017. "California's Cap-and-Trade Program Could Offer Other States Guidance." *The Washington Post*, July 29, 2017. [cited February 4, 2018]. Available from www.washingtonpost.com/opinions/californias-cap-and-trade-program-could-offer-other-states-guidance/2017/07/28/80aadf4c-6e4c-11e7-96ab-5f38140b38cc_story.html?utm_term=.264d2973219.

Waxman, Henry, and with Joshua Green. 2009. *The Waxman Report: How Congress Really Works.* New York: Twelve: Hachette Book Group.

Weisman, Jonathan, and Jennifer Steinhauer. 2013. "Senate Women Lead in Effort to Find Accord." *The New York Times*, October 14, 2013. [cited December 19, 2017]. Available from www.nytimes.com/2013/10/15/us/senate-women-lead-in-effort-to-find-accord.html?mcubz=0.

Welsh, Nick. 2017. "Jackson, Limon on Opposite Sides of Cap-and-Trade Vote." *The Santa Barbara Independent*, July 20, 2017. [cited February 4, 2018]. Available from www.independent.com/news/2017/jul/20/jackson-limon-opposite-sides-cap-and-trade-vote/.

Westwood, Sean J. 2014. "When Bipartisanship Is Partisan: The Strategic Use of Bipartisanship in Congress." Dartmouth University.

White, Margaret Kimbrell, and Sasha Borowsky. 2018. "You Won't Believe the Names the Left if Calling 'No Labels'." *The Wall Street Journal*, April 8, 2018. [cited April 13, 2018]. Available from www.wsj.com/articles/you-wont-believe-the-names-the-left-is-calling-no-labels-1523209037.

Wildermuth, John. 2017. "Feinstein Answers Questions; Still Gets Hard Time from Protesters." *SF Gate*, February 24, 2017. [cited March 26, 2018]. Available from www.sfgate.com/politics/article/Feinstein-answers-questions-still-gets-hard-10957888.php.

Wilderness Connect. 2019. *Wilderness Data Search*. Wilderness Connect 2019. [cited March 18, 2019]. Available from www.wilderness.net/NWPS/advSearch.

Wildlife Management Institute. 2011. "House and Senate Square Off on Federal Budget." [cited October 25, 2017]. Available from www.wildlifemanagementinstitute.org/index.php?option=com_content&view=article&id=516:house-and-senate-square-off-on-federal-budget&catid=34:ONB%20Articles&Itemid=54.

Willon, Phil. 2017. "California Tea Party Conservatives Take Shots at GOP Establishment, Sounding Downright Progressive." *Los Angeles Times*, August 11, 2017. [cited February 4, 2018]. Available from www.latimes.com/politics/essential/la-pol-ca-essential-politics-updates-california-tea-party-takes-shots-at-gop-1502494930-htmlstory.html.

Wolak, Jennifer. 2013. "Congressional Decision-Making and Public Support for Compromise." Paper presented at the *Annual Meeting of the American Political Science Association*. Chicago.

2017a. "Public Expectations of State Legislators." *Legislative Studies Quarterly* 42 (2): 175–209.

2017b. "Support for Compromise in Principle and in Practice." Paper presented at the *Annual Meeting of the American Political Science Association*. San Francisco.

Workman, Samuel, Bryan D. Jones, and Ashley E. Jochim. 2009. "Information Processing and Policy Dynamics." *Policy Studies Journal* 37 (1): 75–92.

Wyant, Sara. 2017. *Lesson #1: Every Farm Bill Is Unique – The Last One Was a Doozy*. AgriPulse, February 2, 2017. [cited December 19, 2017]. Available from www.agri-pulse.com/articles/8894-lesson-1-every-farm-bill-is-unique-the-last-one-was-a-doozy.

Zapler, Mike. 2012. "Lugar Unloads on 'Unrelenting' Partisanship." *Politico*, May 9, 2012. [cited July 3, 2012]. Available from www.politico.com/blogs/on-congress/2012/05/lugar-unloads-on-unrelenting-partisanship-122891.

Zartman, I. William, and Maureen R. Berman. 1982. *The Practical Negotiator*. New Haven: Yale University Press.

Zornick, George. 2014. *Elizabeth Warren Reveals Inside Details of Trade Talks*. The Nation, May 15, 2014. [cited September 5, 2017]. Available from www.thenation.com/article/elizabeth-warren-reveals-inside-details-trade-talks/.

Index

Note: Page numbers in italic and bold refer to figures and tables, respectively.